THE SPREADSHEET
STYLE MANUAL

THE SPREADSHEET STYLE MANUAL

David Harrison   John W. Yu

BUSINESS ONE IRWIN
Homewood, Illinois 60430

This publication is designed to provide accurate and
authoritative information in regard to the subject matter
covered. It is sold with the understanding that neither the
author nor the publisher is engaged in rendering legal, accounting,
or other professional service. If legal advice or other expert
assistance is required, the services of a competent
professional person should be sought.

*From a Declaration of Principles jointly adopted by a Committee
of the American Bar Association and a Committee of Publishers.*

Sponsoring editor: Susan Glinert Stevens, Ph.D.
Project editor: Joan A. Hopkins
Production manager: Ann Cassady
Compositor: Publication Services, Inc.
Typeface: 11/13 Melior
Printer: R. R. Donnelley & Sons Company

Library of Congress Cataloging-in-Publication Data

Harrison, David
    The spreadsheet style manual / David Harrison, John W. Yu.
      p. cm.
    ISBN 1-55623-267-5
    1. Electronic spreadsheets—Handbooks, manuals, etc. 2. Lotus
1-2-3 (Computer program)—Handbooks, manuals, etc. 3. Microsoft
Excel (Computer program)—Handbooks, manuals, etc. 4. Supercalc5
(Computer program)—Handbooks, manuals, etc. I. Yu, John W.
II. Title.
HF5548.2.H377 1990
650'.028'5536—dc20   89–49201
                                          CIP

Printed in the United States of America

2 3 4 5 6 7 8 9 0 DO 7 6 5 4 3 2 1 0

Trademarks

The following are trademarks or registered trademarks for the company indicated. This information has been obtained from a variety of sources; however, its accuracy, adequacy, or completeness cannot be guaranteed.

Apple Computer, Inc.	Apple, Macintosh
Ashton-Tate Corporation	Framework III
Computer Associates International, Inc.	SuperCalc4, SuperCalc5
Funk Software, Inc.	Allways, Noteworthy, Sideways
Hercules Computer Technology	Hercules
Hewlett-Packard Company	HP, LaserJet
International Business Machines Corporation	IBM, CGA, EGA, MCGA, VGA
Lotus Development Corporation	1-2-3
Microsoft Corporation	Excel, Microsoft, MS-DOS
New England Software, Inc.	Graph-in-the-Box
Software Publishing Corporation	Harvard Graphics

Preface

THE PURPOSES OF THIS MANUAL

This manual has two purposes. The first is to provide a set of much needed *standards* for the layout, formatting, and editing of all types of computer-based spreadsheets. In this respect, the book can be used as a reference manual. The second purpose is to provide *guidelines* for spreadsheet users as they set up new spreadsheets and maintain or revise others. In this respect the book can serve as a tutorial. Together, the standards and guidelines make up what we have called *spreadsheet style.*

Good spreadsheet style is clear and effective. To be clear, a spreadsheet must record and communicate information that is accurate, and the immediate meaning of the data must be unambiguous. To be effective, the spreadsheet itself should have a purpose, and that purpose should then be achieved by the manner in which cells, formulas, functions, macros, and other features of the software are used.

Whether used as a reference, as a tutorial, or for both purposes, this manual will help readers improve their spreadsheet style.

The manual can be used along with any computer hardware: microcomputer, minicomputer, or mainframe. It can be used with standalone PC or Macintosh computers, or in a network environment. Most references to printing apply equally to dot matrix, daisywheel, inkjet, or laser output. The techniques described and illustrated are not hardware-dependent.

HOW THE BOOK IS ILLUSTRATED

This is not a book of dry principles, or a tedious progression of checklists, or a set of do's and don'ts. It is designed as a practical no-nonsense manual for the serious spreadsheet user who wants to see immediate results.

Throughout the book, readers will find the standards and guidelines of spreadsheet style illustrated by realistic extracts from professional-level spreadsheets.

The information in the manual is applicable to *any spreadsheet software or integrated program.* The majority of the realistic examples in the book use the most popular spreadsheet program, *Lotus 1-2-3.* In some sections, features from *Microsoft Excel* and *Super-Calc5* are used to illustrate particular aspects of style, such as dialog boxes and graphics, that are particularly well implemented in those programs. However, almost all the techniques described in the manual can be readily adapted to whatever spreadsheet you use at work or home.

Lotus 1-2-3 is the leading character-based spreadsheet program. Since the majority of readers will be familiar with Release 2.01, this version will be used in most examples. Release 3.0 will be used to demonstrate advanced techniques such as three-dimensional spreadsheets and linking of multiple spreadsheets.

Microsoft Excel is a graphics-based spreadsheet program. It will be used to illustrate spreadsheet design features such as dialog boxes that are not available on 1-2-3. SuperCalc5, from Computer Associates International, has been used to illustrate some features of spreadsheet graphics.

All three programs are in wide use in commerce, industry, home-based businesses, government, and universities on mainframe and microcomputer environments. However, if you work with one of the dozens of other excellent spreadsheet programs, you will find it just as easy to apply the style principles from this manual to your favorite program.

WHO THIS MANUAL IS WRITTEN FOR

This manual is written for any spreadsheet user who is looking for some authoritative guidance as to what makes for clear, effective spreadsheet style.

The material has been compiled to answer the needs of the individual spreadsheet user at several levels of expertise:

- Newcomers to the world of spreadsheets will find their priority needs met in the initial sections on spreadsheet style and structure, the basics of spreadsheet planning, and the elements of spreadsheet style, such as layout, block design, and the time-saving use of named ranges.

- Intermediate and advanced users will find specific sections of particulat interest, such as those on cell referencing, formula construction, cell protection, and the effective use of special functions, macros, and spreadsheet linking.

- Users who have already achieved a satisfactory spreadsheet style but are looking for ways to improve their presentation to others will find the sections on graphics, databases, and printing of particular value.

The standards and guidelines in the manual will be of particular value to people who exchange information in spreadsheet form within workgroups, departments, or corporations. One reason for the universal popularity of the computer-based spreadsheet is its free-form flexibility, enabling the user to enter and manipulate virtually any information that lends itself to row-and-column format. But when spreadsheets have to be communicated, shared, and, in some cases, combined with others, this complete freedom of style is not always desirable. With the increase of computer networking, it is often essential to agree on what spreadsheet style is to be followed by the workgroup.

In summary, the intended readership of the book consists of business and professional spreadsheet users. Whatever their level of expertise with spreadsheets, readers will be able to put the standards and guidelines of spreadsheet style to immediate practical use.

HOW THIS MANUAL IS ORGANIZED

The manual is divided into 14 chapters. Chapters 1 to 4 cover the essentials of spreadsheet structure, design, and planning; many readers will want to read these chapters as a unit. Chapters 5 through 13 each present a self-contained treatment of specific aspects of spreadsheet style. These chapters may be read in any order. Chapter 14 brings together some of the key ideas on style from each of the foregoing chapters and offers some concluding advice. A comprehensive subject index completes the manual.

Within each chapter of the manual, the material has been divided into topics, numbered for ease of cross-reference. Thus, to find a topic of interest, you can either start at the Table of Contents, which lists all topics and their page numbers, or you can refer to the subject index and look up the page number that way. Here is a closer look at what you will find in the manual.

Chapter 1:   Spreadsheet Style and Structure

This chapter starts with a true-to-life example of what can easily happen when a spreadsheet is not properly designed. An improved version of the same spreadsheet is then presented, and a list of common-sense standards and guidelines developed. This list serves as a preview of the rest of the manual and gives the reader an idea of what to expect in the chapters that follow.

Chapter 2:   Basic Spreadsheet Planning

This chapter first identifies the characteristics of good spreadsheet style: accuracy, readability, and consistency. The reader is then shown how to plan a spreadsheet to suit the intended user and meet the intended purpose of the presentation. Some limitations of spreadsheets are explained.

Chapter 3:   Block Designs

This chapter sets out the basic standards and guidelines for effective spreadsheet design and style, for instance

- What is a good spreadsheet layout?
- Where should you locate the data, the calculations, and the macros?
- Where is the best place to put formulas?
- How can you document your spreadsheets and explain them to others?

The concept of block design is introduced and illustrated. Readers are shown how to set up simple block designs in which to locate spreadsheet documentation, input, calculation, output, and macros.

Chapter 4: Inside the Spreadsheet Blocks

Specific guidelines are presented for setting up the various blocks of the spreadsheet. Examples are used to show typical contents of the design blocks suggested in Chapter 3.

Chapter 5: Cell Addresses and Referencing

This chapter explains the use of relative, absolute, and mixed cell reference in spreadsheet formulas. Examples are provided to illustrate how to design spreadsheets so that changes to data require minimal changes to the spreadsheet formulas. Guidelines are provided for the use of circular references and named ranges.

Chapter 6: Documenting and Protecting Cell Contents

This chapter sets out guidelines for documenting formulas in cells either on printouts or through the use of cell notes. Illustrations include cell noting add-in programs. Techniques for printing spreadsheet formulas are described.

Chapter 7: Error Checking Techniques

This chapter explains how to locate spreadsheet design errors such as circular cell references and abnormal cell formulas. Standard error techniques described include: check of row and column totals, check of input values, and check of missing values.

Chapter 8: Decision-Making Style: Using IF, CHOOSE and Table Lookup

This chapter provides guidelines for the most effective use of three functions used to build decision-making into a spreadsheet: standard and nested IF functions, the CHOOSE function, and the variants of table lookup.

Chapter 9: Macros, Menus, and User-Defined Functions

This chapter explains how to design macros that work without error and are easy to change. The basic form of macro design is explained. Specific recommendations are made on naming variables used in macros, as well as routines for tidying up after macro execution. Guidelines are also provided for the design of menus, dialog boxes, and user-defined functions.

Chapter 10:   Multiple, Linked, and 3-D Spreadsheets

This chapter provides guidelines for the design and style of multiple spreadsheets. Proper design of linked and three-dimensional spreadsheets is also described and illustrated. Criteria are set out to help the user decide when each type of spreadsheet is appropriate.

Chapter 11:   Style for Spreadsheet Databases

This chapter deals with points of style for databases implemented on a spreadsheet, an application often used for personnel, inventory, or mailing lists. The reader is shown how to adapt the block design approach to serve these purposes. Guidelines are provided for setting up input, output, and criteria blocks, as well as for the use of features such as named ranges.

Chapter 12:   Style for Spreadsheet Graphics

This chapter explains how to design spreadsheets that can easily be linked to graphs for analysis or presentation. It includes a brief overview of common graph types, guidelines for the general use of graphics, as well as guidelines for setting up spreadsheet text and data for ease of transfer to the graphic display.

Chapter 13:   Spreadsheet Printing and Publishing

This chapter presents standards for the design of presentation-quality spreadsheets in printed form. Guidelines are presented for printing large spreadsheets, for printing sideways, and for desktop publishing. This chapter will be of value to readers with any kind of printer.

Chapter 14:   In a Few Words . . .

This brief chapter presents a selection of the key ideas of each chapter and three final words that together synthesize the meaning of good style.

A subject index is provided.

ACKNOWLEDGMENTS

The idea for this book emerged from the keen interest shown in spreadsheet style by scores of participants in our business and professional development seminars. It crystallised into *The Spreadsheet Style Manual* thanks to senior editor Susan Glinert's urging us to write a slender manual that people would really use. We thank her as well as the reviewers and the editorial and production staff at Business One Irwin for the expertise (and style) they brought to the project.

For our families, as always, we cannot find enough words to express our gratitude for their support and understanding.

As for our confidence that this is a manual that people will really use, now it's up to you!

David Harrison

John W. Yu

Contents

List of Figures

THE SPREADSHEET
STYLE MANUAL

CHAPTER ONE

Spreadsheet Style and Structure

Eight million users can't be wrong. Spreadsheet programs are easy to learn, easy to use, and show results fast. Eight million users? This is the ballpark number of accountants and artisans, bankers and bookkeepers, presidents, technopeasants, and all manner of other people who have been using spreadsheets since these programs first took off in popularity around 1983.

The indisputable fact, though, is that the concept of the electronic spreadsheet is very straightforward. You do your work on a simple framework, or matrix of rows and columns. As the rows and columns intersect, they form cells. In spreadsheet terms, a cell can contain a value (that is, a number), some text (words), or a formula (a coded instruction to do a calculation).

The most evident power of a spreadsheet is its speed of calculation. Change one number in a typical spreadsheet, for example the price of some product, a weekly wage, or a discount rate, and quicker than you can say "Return," all cells on the spreadsheet affected by that number are recalculated and new values are shown.

It is hardly surprising, therefore, that so many users have rushed to take advantage of this new medium, adapting it to a broad range of financial and other applications, but without paying too much attention to the way in which their work is arranged on the spreadsheet. Perhaps something similar happened with the invention of paper or the birth of radio. It was just so satisfying to be able to write on paper or transmit words and music by radio, that people for some time probably got along quite well without many standards or guidelines about what they wanted to write, speak, or play, let alone how they wanted to *arrange* it. Yet now we have in every language and culture a certain agreement amongst the users of paper and the radio waves: agreement not so much about *what* can be communicated, but about *how* it is communicated.

So it is with spreadsheets. The premise of this book is that the way you put those values and text and formulas together into an entity that conveys useful information is equally as important as the content of your spreadsheet.

We have chosen the word "style" to express a particular way of working with the content of a spreadsheet. We believe that, just as a good writer uses a certain style to engage, inform, and persuade the reader, so can a spreadsheet developer use style to communicate data, assist in problem solving, and provide the raw material for decision making.

In this book, we are going to build upon what you already know. For you already know something—perhaps a lot—about spreadsheets. If you are using spreadsheets for business purposes, well, of course you know plenty about your business. You also know about style, for as a writer and a speaker, you have developed a style of your own; and whether you are an observer or a participant, you may know how important style is to an artist, a sports competitor, or a politician. Cynics have even said that in politics, style is everything.

1.1 THE VALUE OF STYLE

But what is it that makes for "good" style? This is a question we shall frequently return to in this book. Our consistent aim will be to offer you brief, practical guidance about what constitutes good style in spreadsheet layout, in the construction of formulas, in documenting macros, in the use of spreadsheet graphics, and so on.

Just before writing this chapter, we looked at what several other authors had thought and written about style. Virtually every manual or article about literary style could be distilled into four words expressing the authors' opinions about the qualities of good style: clarity, brevity, consistency, and sincerity.

Clarity, brevity, and consistency will certainly be recurring themes in this manual of spreadsheet style. Sincerity? If sincerity of writing means validity and truth, then this characteristic of style is equally desirable in spreadsheets.

Certain types of spreadsheets, particularly in business, financial, or research circumstances are referred to as models; that is, the data—and perhaps accompanying graphics—represent a model of a real-world situation (such as the state of a business or the forecast for an investment). So if spreadsheets are to be models of reality, then they must be valid models. Unless our input data represent the truth of the matter, the resulting output data—and all decisions that flow from that information—will be of little use to anyone. As the jingle goes, "Garbage In, Garbage Out." We must, therefore, use our wits to construct valid, reliable, error-free spreadsheets.

This is precisely why style is of value. The consistent use of good spreadsheet style will significantly reduce the chance of error. Spreadsheets that do not observe certain key standards of style can very easily contain error. These errors often occur in the underlying formulas used in calculating the spreadsheet. As the actual formulas are seldom printed with business reports, errors in them may remain hidden from all but the most careful user. Frequently, the errors are not spotted by anyone, and the faulty data presented in the spreadsheet lead to equally faulty conclusions and bad business decisions.

The true story in the following example illustrates the kind of problem that can easily occur as the result of careless spreadsheet style.

Example 1.

A company was considering the acquisition of another business. It made sense to management to engage a large accounting firm to evaluate the merits of the proposed acquisition. The accounting firm was given the relevant data and a set of assumptions; these assumptions included expected interest rates and inflation rates, projected sales growth, probable cash collections, and so on. The purchase of the business would cost over $20 million.

The accounting firm assigned an accountant with business valuation experience (and an apparently good working knowledge of spreadsheet programs) to prepare the report on the proposed acquisition. He developed some complex spreadsheets to assist in the evaluation, including pro forma financial statements, cash flow projections, and debt service schedules.

At various points in the analysis, the accountant consulted the client about the various assumptions the company had made in the spreadsheets. It was a period of fluctuating interest rates. As a result, the accountant made several changes to the assumptions, including the expected interest rate. After several weeks of painstaking work, the results of the analysis were ready. The spreadsheet analysis showed that the acquisition was going to be a profitable venture.

On the day before the final report was to be presented to the client, the senior partner reviewed the report with the accountant in charge of the assignment. He asked questions such as "Were the spreadsheet models correctly constructed?" and "Have they been carefully tested?" Looking at the spreadsheet printouts, the senior partner had an uneasy feeling that something about the spreadsheet figures did not match the hard facts of the actual business situation.

Sure enough, after several hours of scrutiny, the senior partner discovered that different rates of interest had been used in several crucial formulas of the spreadsheets. This made no sense at all. Unfortunately, all the interest rates had been built into the formulas of the spreadsheets. When the accountant had changed the interest rate assumption, he had changed some of the values in the formulas but overlooked others.

Once the correct interest rates were substituted in the formulas, the entire spreadsheet model was reviewed. It showed that the client firm would *lose* a lot of money from the proposed acquisition. The recommendation should therefore have been *not* to go ahead with the acquisition.

Fortunately, the senior partner's experience and careful audit of the report saved the accounting firm from a costly lawsuit that could have resulted from the incorrectly based recommendation. In summary, the accountant had failed to observe a very important rule of spreadsheet style.

> If a critical value, such as an interest rate, is used in different cells of a spreadsheet, then show it in a separate cell that is clearly labeled. Do not embed it in formulas. Instead, formulas requiring use of the critical value should reference the cell containing the critical value.

This example demonstrates the importance not only of proper spreadsheet style, but also the value of questioning the assumptions made in the construction of any spreadsheet.

FIGURE 1–1a Income Projection (Three-Month Spreadsheet)

	A	B	C	D
		Jan 90	Feb 90	Mar 90
1				
2				
3	Revenue from sales	$200,000	$210,000	$220,000
4				
5	Expenses:			
6	Store rent	19,000	19,700	20,400
7	Selling expenses	24,000	25,200	26,400
8	Wages and benefits	85,000	85,000	85,000
9	Advertising	10,000	10,000	10,000
10	Other expenses	5,000	5,000	5,000
11		-------------	-------------	-------------
12	Total expenses	143,000	144,900	146,800
13		-------------	-------------	-------------
14	Net income	$57,000	$65,100	$73,200
15		=============	=============	=============

Example 2.

Figures 1–1a and 1–1b show a partial spreadsheet that includes not only an embedded interest rate problem similar to Example 1, but also a number of other points of dubious spreadsheet style. They may not necessarily be errors as such, but each of these points of style adds to an overall impression of a spreadsheet that has been left unfinished. Some of the loose ends in this spreadsheet could easily trip up a later user of the spreadsheet.

This *Lotus 1-2-3* spreadsheet calculates the projected income for Milwaukee Discount Electronics (MDE) for the first three months of 1990. Figure 1–1a displays the computed results of the spreadsheet. Figure 1–1b displays the underlying formulas. Only the formulas for January and February are shown, those for March being similar.

MDE rents a store and pays a base monthly rent of $5,000 plus 7 percent of its sales to the landlord. The monthly selling expense is projected to be 12 percent of sales revenue.

This spreadsheet exhibits several problems of spreadsheet style, including the treatment of common data and the need for titles.

Common Data. The store rent (row 6) is calculated with the 7 percent on sales shown as a number in the formulas. Similarly, the selling expenses (row 7) are calculated using a predicted rate of 12 percent (of sales), shown as a number in the formulas. Any change to these percentages will require changes to every formula in rows 6 and 7.

FIGURE 1–1*b*   Income Projection (Formulas for Two Months)

	A	B	C
1		Jan 90	Feb 90
2			
3	Revenue from sales	200000	210000
4			
5	Expenses:		
6	Store rent	5000+.07*B3	5000+.07*C3
7	Selling expenses	+B3*.12	+C3*.12
8	Wages and benefits	85000	85000
9	Advertising	10000	10000
10	Other expenses	5000	5000
11		------------	------------
12	Total expenses	@SUM(B6:B10)	@SUM(C6:C10)
13		------------	------------
14	Net income	+B3-B12	+C3-C12
15		============	============

Titles.   Another deficiency is that the spreadsheet is not properly titled. Without a title, there is no immediate indication what the spreadsheet is about.

Example 3.

Figures 1–2*a* and 1–2*b* show an edited version of the Milwaukee income projections for MDE from Example 2, incorporating several improvements in spreadsheet style. (Only the first three months of values and two months' formulas are shown.) Comparing the original and revised spreadsheets, you will notice several improvements.

Date.   The original date the spreadsheet was prepared and the date the spreadsheet was last revised are clearly shown.

User.   The intended readership of the spreadsheet is identified.

Developer.   The developer of the spreadsheet is named.

Assumptions.   The rental royalty is placed in cell C8, and clearly indicated using the label in cell A8. The percentage of sales for selling expenses is placed in cell C9, and clearly labeled in cell A9.

Title.   The spreadsheet is clearly titled, showing (in rows 11 to 13) that the spreadsheet calculates the projected income for MDE for January to June, 1990.

FIGURE 1–2a Improved Income Projection (Three-Month Spreadsheet)

	A	B	C	D
1	Date prepared:	11/10/89		
2	Date revised:	11/21/89		
3	User:	M. Romanski, Manager		
4	Developer:	F. Bezemer		
5	Purpose:	Income projection		
6				
7	Assumptions:			
8	Rental royalty as percent of sales		7.00%	
9	Selling expenses as percent of sales		12.00%	
10	--			
11		Milwaukee Discount Electronics		
12		Income Projection		
13		For the period Jan 90 to Jun 90		
14				
15		Jan 90	Feb 90	Mar 90
16				
17	Revenue from sales	$200,000	$210,000	$220,000
18				
19	Expenses:			
20	Store rent	19,000	19,700	20,400
21	Selling expenses	24,000	25,200	26,400
22	Wages and benefits	85,000	85,000	85,000
23	Advertising	10,000	10,000	10,000
24	Other expenses	5,000	5,000	5,000
25		-------------------------------		
26	Total expenses	143,000	144,900	146,800
27		-------------------------------		
28	Net income	$57,000	$65,100	$73,200
29		===============================		

Relationships.   The row labels are indented to show the relationships between the various rows.

Formulas.   The percentage in cell C8 is referenced in the formulas in row 20 (store rent). Similarly, the percentage in cell C9 is referenced in row 21 (selling expenses). Thus, a change in any of the two percentage figures can be effected by changing the value in cell C8 or C9 without needing to change any of the formulas in the spreadsheet. Note that the formulas that reference cells C8 and C9 could be constructed using absolute references to facilitate the copying of formulas from one month to the next.

1.2 GUIDELINES FOR THE STRUCTURE OF A SPREADSHEET

Using the preceding examples, we can generalize an initial set of guidelines for the structure of a spreadsheet.

FIGURE 1-2*b*   Improved Income Projection (Formulas for Two Months)

```
                          A                                    B                          C
1    Date prepared:                          @DATE(11,10,89)
2    Date revised:                           @DATE(11,21,89)
3    User:                                   M. Romanski, Manager
4    Developer:                              F. Bezemer
5    Purpose:                                Income projection
6
7    Assumptions:
8    Rental royalty as percent of sales                      0.07
9    Selling expenses as percent of sales                    0.12
10   ----------------------------------------------------------------
11                                           Milwaukee Discount Electronics
12                                                  Income Projection
13                                           For the period Jan 90 to Jun 90
14
15                                           Jan 90               Feb 90
16
17   Revenue from sales                      200000               210000
18
19   Expenses:
20       Store rent                          5000+C8*B17          5000+C8*C17
21       Selling expenses                    +B17*C9              +C17*C9
22       Wages and benefits                  85000                85000
23       Advertising                         10000                10000
24       Other expenses                      5000                 5000
25                                           --------------       --------------
26           Total expenses                  @SUM(B20:B24)        @SUM(C20:C24)
27                                           --------------       --------------
28   Net income                              +B17-B26             +C17-C26
29                                           ==============       ==============
```

Date.   A spreadsheet should include date information: both the original creation date and the subsequent revision date should be clearly identified.

User.   Just like a report, if a spreadsheet is created for use by someone other than its developer, the user should be clearly identified on the spreadsheet.

Developer.   The developer, or "owner," of the spreadsheet should be noted so that queries about it can be directed to the right person.

Title and labels.   The spreadsheet should be clearly titled and labeled. The name of the business, the purpose of the spreadsheet, and the time period, activities, or departments covered by the spreadsheet should be clearly shown on the spreadsheet.

Relationships.   Columns and rows of values should be clearly labeled. In the case of row labels, appropriate use of indentation can clarify the relationship between the rows.

Assumptions.   Any common data value used by more than one formula should be extracted from the formulas and placed in a common data area so that changes can be applied to the data area without necessitating changes to the formulas.

Totals.   Following the practice of accountants, any subtotal in columns should be preceded by a ruled line to indicate that the value represents the sum of the values above the line. Similarly, a total should also be preceded by a line. It is a customary practice to underscore a total value by a double underline.

Units.   The unit of measure should be clearly identified using appropriate formats. For example, if an amount in a cell is a percentage, format the cell to display the amount in percent. If an amount in a cell is a dollar amount, format the cell to display the amount in the cell with leading dollar sign, and embedded commas to separate thousands. It is an accepted practice to only show the dollar sign for the first and last value in a column if all the values in the column are dollar amounts.

Filename.   An appropriate filename should be used for the file in which the spreadsheet is to be stored. Try to name spreadsheets in such a way that the filename provides some clue as to the purpose of the spreadsheet.

File directories.   Organize directories in a logical manner so that related spreadsheets are stored in their own subdirectory. For example, you may create a subdirectory called \BUDGET and store all spreadsheets that deal with budget information in this subdirectory. If you are using diskettes, save related spreadsheets on a single diskette.

In the chapters that follow, there are many more guidelines for various aspects of spreadsheet style. Chapter 2 covers the basics of spreadsheet planning, leading naturally into the material on block designs in Chapter 3. Then in Chapter 4, you will find specific ideas for the contents of these major spreadsheet blocks. You may read or reference any topic or chapter of the manual separately from the others. Cross-references have been added to assist you.

CHAPTER TWO

Basic Spreadsheet Planning

Because a spreadsheet is so easy to change, it is very tempting to start building a spreadsheet from scratch, without a clear plan of where all the data, calculations, and results are to go. Many people, in fact, prefer to work directly on a blank spreadsheet screen, entering values, formulas, titles, and labels more or less as they come to mind, doing a bit of formatting here and there. The plan evolves as they go. Most often, they end up with a spreadsheet that, at least for them, does what it was designed to do. For a simple spreadsheet with only a few dozen cells and a short life ahead, this expedient approach may be quite acceptable. Readers who already work this way and are satisfied with it may prefer to skip this chapter on planning, and move ahead to other, more specific chapters of this style manual.

A planned approach, however, may be preferable if any of the following conditions apply.

- The spreadsheet is to be used by someone other than the original developer.

- The spreadsheet is large, complex, or has many interrelated cells and formulas.

- The spreadsheet is to be used formally in a written or oral presentation, even to a small workgroup.

- The spreadsheet is to be used repeatedly, updated, adapted, or combined with other information.

This chapter presents a planned approach to spreadsheet development. It first sets out characteristics of good spreadsheet design (Section 2.1), then describes a way to plan a spreadsheet in terms of the users' needs (Section 2.2), the specific purposes of the spreadsheet (Section 2.3), and the nature of the actual data (Section 2.4). Adapting existing spreadsheets and creating templates is the next topic (Section 2.5). Finally, a spreadsheet program may not always be the best medium for setting up and solving a numerical problem; so we end this chapter by defining some limitations of which the planner should be aware (Section 2.6).

2.1 CHARACTERISTICS OF GOOD SPREADSHEET DESIGN

Before building (or acquiring) anything that has a design to it, most people have a fairly clear idea about the characteristics of "good" design. For instance, when you shop for a car, you already know from experience that the essential characteristics of a car include safety, reliability, comfort, durability, and, of course, mobility. You may or may not be concerned with other design features such as aerodynamic profile, fuel efficiency, speed, or ease of maintenance. Similarly, you probably have a pretty fair idea about what, for you, represents a good design of a house, a boat, a suit for the office, or a better mousetrap.

Now, what makes for a good spreadsheet? Undoubtedly, the number one priority is for it "to work." The spreadsheet must work for its intended purpose and meet the needs of its users.

A good, workable spreadsheet also exhibits the characteristics of *accuracy*, *readability*, and *consistency*. The developer of a spreadsheet can do a lot to enhance these qualities. Indeed, the improvement of accuracy, readability, is the essence of this book about spreadsheet style.

This section takes up each of the three characteristics in turn, defines them, and suggests ways developers can build these qualities into their spreadsheets. Numerous forward references are made to other sections of this manual.

Accuracy. This means more than just ensuring the accuracy of source data and the correct setup of formulas. It also means that the developer has provided the user with a trouble-free means of entering the data in the spreadsheet. In addition, good spreadsheet style calls for the ability to *audit* (that is, verify) that the data are, indeed, accurately entered and the cells correctly related. Either the developer or the end user may need to trace the means by which the spreadsheet produces its results. Most often, the audit of a spreadsheet is largely visual: checking the underlying formulas and ensuring they make sense individually. But there are other ways to build in the audit of relationships between cells and to ensure that computation proceeds without fault.

Features of spreadsheet style that improve accuracy include:

- Input screens or dialog boxes for data prompt and data entry (Sections 4.2, 9.5 and 9.6).

- Circular references clearly identified, and the reason for their use documented in the spreadsheet (Sections 5.6 to 5.9).

- Cell notes and other documentation of critical values and formulas to clarify the internal design of the spreadsheet (Chapter 6).

- Built-in error checking of data by comparing row and column totals; accountants call this cross-footing (Section 7.1).

- Macros to prompt for data input and to check the validity of the data at the point of entry (Section 7.2).

- For linked, multiple, and 3-D spreadsheets, the purpose and rationale for the links, as well as specific identification of the linked cells and ranges (Chapter 10).

Readability. Readability of any report is affected by factors such as visual appearance, organization of content, length of words and sentences, complexity of concepts, and the way the writer has taken into account the knowledge and needs of the reader. A spreadsheet, being a special kind of report, is affected by similar readability factors.

Readability is also enhanced by good documentation. This documentation can clearly indicate the purpose, the assumptions, and any important information about values or formulas in the spreadsheet.

Features of spreadsheet style that improve readability include:

- Content that is logically organized into separate visual blocks, such as documentation, variable data or assumptions, calculations, and results (Chapters 3 and 4).

- Organization of the spreadsheet blocks so that cell ranges that are to be viewed together fit into the physical limitation of the conventional screen (Chapter 3).

- Meaningful spreadsheet titles, row labels, and column headings (Section 4.1).

- Use of straightforward concepts and terminology wherever possible; specific definition of any terms that might be unclear or ambiguous to a user (Section 4.1).

- Formulas that are concise and readily understandable, rather than so long that they constantly overrun the borders of cells and pages; formula length controlled by using intermediate calculations (Section 4.3).

- A visual appearance that is open and uncluttered by extraneous detail; judicious use of fonts, rules, and other typographic features (Chapter 13).

Consistency. This characteristic is associated with the ideas of reliability and confidence. A consistent style in a spreadsheet will produce reliable results in which the user can place a high degree of confidence. Spreadsheet design features that improve consistency include:

- Consistent use of terminology in headings, labels, category names, graph labels, and documentation.

- Assumptions about the spreadsheet model listed to help the user determine the applicability of the model for a specific situation (Section 4.1).

- Named ranges used in formulas to help identify data, speed up cell references, and reduce the risk of error in citing cell references (Sections 5.10 and 5.11).

- Special spreadsheet functions such as ERR and NA to indicate erroneous or missing values (Chapter 7).

- Proper use of IF, CHOOSE, and table lookup functions to improve spreadsheet decision making and further reduce the risk of error (Chapter 8).

2.2 PLANNING A SPREADSHEET FOR THE USER

There are really two phases of planning a spreadsheet.

1. Thinking through a few basic questions about the use and purpose of the spreadsheet.

2. Spending a few minutes with paper, pencil, and a simple electronic calculator to work out a block design for the

spreadsheet. The idea is to know roughly how your spreadsheet will look and how it will work *before* you switch on the computer and load the program (or, if you are at a terminal, before you log on). We do not, of course, mean that you laboriously write out the whole spreadsheet first on paper— only that you set up a block design or map of where all the parts of the spreadsheet will go.

For effective spreadsheet planning two major questions should be considered and answered: Who will use the spreadsheet? What is the purpose of the spreadsheet?

Whether a spreadsheet is going to be used primarily by the developer or by other users can make a difference in the way it is designed. A spreadsheet designed for others to use should generally have more structure and formality. Assumptions must be clearly stated, preferably in a special block of the spreadsheet. Any ambiguity, whatever the source, must be anticipated and corrected. The technical background, level of experience, and general frame of reference of the user must be taken into account.

A spreadsheet intended only for one's own use requires less formality, but can often benefit as well from attention to the design features described in this chapter. As a spreadsheet is adapted and becomes more complex, the value of having an organized structure becomes evident at all levels of use.

2.3 PLANNING FOR SPECIFIC PURPOSES

What problem is the spreadsheet designed to solve? Is the spreadsheet used for calculating the monthly payment for a car loan, or calculating income tax payable, or planning next year's cash requirements? If the spreadsheet serves more than one purpose, making a list of the purposes could help to sort out relevant from irrelevant data.

Four typical purposes of spreadsheets are described in this section. Such specialized spreadsheets are often described as *models*, that is, the simulation of a process or problem to analyze present conditions or predict future outcomes.

Record keeping and calculation. This is the most basic spreadsheet model, and it provides for a display of quantitative information on some operation or task. Simple arithmetic processes such as addition, subtraction, multiplication, division, and exponentiation can then be applied to those values. The problem and the formulas used in the model are relatively simple. The output is probably in the form of new values.

Examples.

- A spreadsheet designed to calculate a schedule of loan payments.

- An inventory spreadsheet containing information about the inventory items and the calculated carrying values.

- An accounts receivable spreadsheet used to track the accounts receivable amounts and to calculate the aging of accounts.

What-if analysis. The what-if model enables the user to project what might happen to a given situation if one or more variables in that situation were changed. This analysis can assist the user to predict the outcome of different scenarios, and to make related decisions. A typical what-if analysis starts with a base model that represents the most realistic estimate of what may happen. Alternative variants of the scenario can be investigated. What-if models must have built-in flexibility. A good what-if spreadsheet will collect all variables (those that may change from scenario to scenario) into a prominent block of spreadsheet cells in which data variables can be changed easily, without disturbing the calculation formulas. (This technique is fully explained in Chapter 3.)

Examples.

- A spreadsheet designed to compare a lease-or-buy option, based on assumptions about the interest rate, the term, and costs. Changes in these data variables would yield different results and decisions.

- A spreadsheet designed to project cash flow requirements of a business, based on assumptions about sales volume, timing and amount of accounts receivable, various uses of cash, and interest rates for investments and loans. The what-if model enables the user to investigate potential cash flow as changes are made to the assumptions.

- A spreadsheet designed for retirement planning, with various assumptions about the frequency and amount of contributions to the plan, the desired age of retirement, the projected life span after retirement, and the inflation rate. Changes to the assumptions of the base model would yield data on which to base different investment strategies.

Sensitivity analysis. This spreadsheet model is used to identify the impact that one specific change can have on a situation in which there are several, or perhaps many, interrelated factors. By estimating the way a situation responds to a particular change (that is, the sensitivity of certain variables), the analyst can determine the margin of error in the decision, and make appropriate allowance. Although what-if analysis usually allows for changes in several variables, sensitivity analysis typically focuses on only one variable. Small changes to this variable may result in drastic changes (thus, high sensitivity). Alternatively, a change in the key variable may produce little overall change (low sensitivity). Sensitivity analysis determines the impact of changes to one variable, holding all other variables constant.

Examples.

- A spreadsheet designed to analyze the impact of the fluctuations of the exchange rate of Japanese yen to U.S. dollars on the cost of components for a television manufacturer who imports most of the electronic components from Japan. Minor fluctuations in the exchange rate may result in major changes in net income. The sensitivity analysis performed using this spreadsheet could shape the amount and timing of forward contracts to protect against foreign exchange fluctuations.

- A spreadsheet designed to analyze the impact of changes in the interest rate on large projects that require large amounts of capital investment. By analyzing the sensitivity of the returns on investment of such projects to changes in the interest rate, the project manager may be able to determine the margin of error required to protect investors.

Goal seeking. In the goal-seeking model, the analyst works backwards from a desired, quantified outcome (the goal) to determine the specific change that would be needed in one variable in order for that goal to be achieved. In spreadsheets, this is achieved by means of *iteration* [described in Section 5.6]. By means of iteration, the model determines the value of one independent variable that would achieve the desired goal. In this sense, goal-seeking models are the reverse of sensitivity analysis.

Examples.

- A spreadsheet designed to determine the range of wage settlements for union employees in order to maintain a certain level of net income. The spreadsheet has a preentered net income amount, and the model iterates until it determines the wage and salary expenses to achieve the net income amount.

- A spreadsheet designed to determine the annual pension plan contributions required to attain a desired lump sum of money at retirement.

2.4 PLANNING FOR THE DATA

What kind of data will be entered in the spreadsheet? In what form?

Constants and variable data. Many spreadsheets comprise essentially two kinds of data—constants and variables. Constant data are values that are unlikely to change as a spreadsheet is updated or modified. Variable data are subject to frequent change. In smaller, short-lived spreadsheets, the distinction may not be too important. Both constants and variables may be included within formulas. This method is fast and requires no special layout skills. However, if the spreadsheet is to be updated several times (such as in a planning budget), variable data should be collected into a common area and those cells referenced by a formula (as in the examples in Chapter 1).

Selection of data. In designing spreadsheets, be vigilant about what data are to be included and what data are to be left out. There is no merit in entering values that are not used in the spreadsheet. Extraneous data hampers the understanding and maintenance of spreadsheets, and makes debugging much harder.

Units of measure. Use standard, clearly defined units of measure. Add labels to clarify the units. For example, if the user is to enter an interest rate in a data cell, make it clear whether the interest rate is to be entered as a whole number (as in 12 for 12 percent), or as a decimal (as in .12 for 12 percent).

Cell formats for data. Set the format of numeric values to conform to standard conventions. Be particularly careful with dollar amounts and quantities: if a dollar value may be mistaken for a quantity, format the value clearly or give it a text label, or both.

If the values in a column of numbers are all dollar amounts, follow the accounting convention of formatting the topmost cell to show the dollar sign, and do the same for any cell that shows totals. Leave the rest of the cells without the dollar signs. For example, in *Lotus 1-2-3*, the Currency format puts the dollar sign at the front, inserts commas between thousands, rounds to a specified number of decimal places, and shows negative values in parentheses. The "comma" format is exactly the same, but omits the dollar sign.

Where values are expressed in thousands of units, include such information in the row or column labels. For example, the label "(in $000s)" indicates that the amounts are in thousands of dollars. Always format amounts (such as interest rates) that are usually expressed as percentages to show the percent sign (%).

Watch out for unclear date formats. For example, two users may have different interpretations of a date shown as 02-05-91. Is it May 2, 1991, or is it February 5, 1991? Wherever possible in a program, select an unambiguous date format such as 02-May-91.

2.5 ADAPTING SPREADSHEETS AND USING TEMPLATES

It is often unnecessary to plan and build a spreadsheet from scratch as there may already be an existing spreadsheet that can be readily adapted and put to work. A spreadsheet that has been carefully developed for a particular one-time use can often be recycled for a similar, but slightly different, business or financial model. A what-if analysis, an income statement, a budget forecast, an amortization table, or chart of stocks and share prices that has been set up with good style may be quite suitable for adaptation to new circumstances and data. Typically, the process is as follows:

- Check the structure, cell relationships, and underlying formulas of the original spreadsheet.

- Check any documentation accompanying the original spreadsheet. Ensure that the design and assumptions of the original fit the new purpose and data.

- Check all formulas to see whether any variable data have been built into them. If so, consider moving the variable data to a separate block of cells and referencing the formula to those cells.

- After adaptation is complete, double check that all necessary changes have been made to titles, headings, labels, and (especially) dates, and that the new spreadsheet is correctly documented.

- Be sure to change the filename!

A special kind of adaptation of an existing spreadsheet model is the *template*. Making a template is an extremely simple and effective technique. It is essentially a spreadsheet from which all the data have been removed: the conventional style is to replace them by zeros. All relevant labels, headings, formulas, and functions remain as the permanent part of the template. Text and formulas not required should be blanked. When the template is set up in this way, some cells with underlying formulas may display ERR conditions, which should disappear as the new data are entered. It is good style to give the base template (that is, the form with the zeros) a distinctive filename, say BUDGTEMP to distinguish it from the various modifications that may be made to it.

Once the user enters new data into the template to replace the zeros, the formulas do their computations, and the spreadsheet is set up for the new situation. Again, remember to save it under a new and unique filename to distinguish it from the base template.

2.6 LIMITATIONS OF SPREADSHEET MODELS

Know the limitations of your spreadsheet program and work within them. Otherwise, what may be a perfect design on paper may not be feasible on-screen. Common limitations of spreadsheet programs include:

Limitations of the spreadsheet window. Most spreadsheet programs can display only 20 rows at a time in a full-screen window. (*Microsoft Excel* and *Lotus 1-2-3* Releases 2.2 and 3 are exceptions, allowing more than 20 rows to be displayed.) The maximum number of columns that can be viewed on-screen depends on the column widths; however, most screens can only display a maximum of 80 characters across the screen.

For example, if the columns are set 9 or 10 characters wide, a matrix of 20 rows by 8 columns can be displayed. Allowing for headings, labels, and rules, it is better to plan for a working area of 15 rows by 5 or 6 columns of actual data. However, large spreadsheets may require special strategies. It is often advisable to break up very large data tables into smaller blocks. Data tables and long formulas that run off the screen generally decrease readability and can increase the risk of error.

Limitations of the row-and-column format. Spreadsheets are designed to work with information that can be presented in rows and fixed columns. Information that does not fit into the row and column format may be better processed by other means, such as word processing, desktop publishing, or freeform outlining software. Some spreadsheet programs are now able to work in three dimensions, providing a new kind of flexibility to the user. [See Chapter 10 for information on multiple, linked, and 3-D spreadsheets.]

Limitations of cell formatting. Many programs offer only a limited measure of control over cell formats. For example, most spreadsheet programs do provide a floating $ format with the dollar sign displayed immediately next to the numbers:

```
    $123.45
  $6,789.12
```

Advanced programs may also permit the left justification of the $ symbol in a column:

```
  $    123.45
  $6,789.12
```

Other formats permitted by advanced programs include American, British, and European date formats; and American, metric, and customized numeric formats.

Limitations of capacity (such as calculation speed). Spreadsheet programs are not efficient in the use of computing resources. If a problem requires a very large number of formula calculations, a spreadsheet program could take several times as long to process the information, compared to a more efficient implementation in a programming language.

Limitations on report writing. Except with advanced spreadsheet programs, it may be difficult to create and format reports of any complexity. For example, it is generally not a simple matter to generate aged receivable reports, customer lists, or client letters from an accounts receivable spreadsheet.

Limitations on complexity. Spreadsheet programs are not always suitable for calculations that require complex logic, mathematical formulas, logical comparisons, or decision branches. Some advanced spreadsheet programs may provide a macro programming language to augment formulas and permit more complex logic. In other cases, it may be better to use a programming language such as BASIC or PASCAL, or to use a database program.

CHAPTER THREE

Block Designs

This chapter proposes a simple method of planning and setting up spreadsheets in a block layout, each block having a very specific purpose in the spreadsheet.

Once you are familiar with this method, you will probably be able to develop the block design on-screen as you enter the details of the spreadsheet. However, initially, and for larger or more complex spreadsheets, it is preferable to first block out the design on paper. A multicolumn pad of worksheets printed for bookkeeping would be useful in this planning phase.

The *block design* is a simple concept that is equally useful for doing a floor plan of a house, setting up to landscape a garden, or sketching a layout for a company brochure. In the beginning, there is an expanse of floor, or land, or paper, and the developer's task is to position on this expanse a manageable number of blocks of housing, or plants and shrubs, or text and graphics. This positioning must be done to achieve some general design goals and an overall effect. The planner, by definition, does not place the blocks at random, but in a way that meets certain objectives of function and, perhaps, art. The way the blocks are placed and the way they act together to produce a particular effect is an important aspect of spreadsheet style.

The four sections of this chapter provide some ideas on how to go about block design:

3.1 Single block design
3.2 Multiple block design

In Chapter 4, we look inside each of the standard spreadsheet blocks and make recommendations for the form and content of those blocks.

3.1 SINGLE BLOCK DESIGN

The simplest block design, suitable for most record keeping or calculation spreadsheets, is a single block. The data and calculations are contained in a range of cells immediately below the title or other introductory heading.

There are two dimensions to this spreadsheet: rows and columns. The main design decision is: Which data should go in the rows, and which data should go in the columns? This decision directly affects the efficiency of the spreadsheet. Some spreadsheet programs have no means to transpose the rows and columns of a spreadsheet; the only way to transpose a spreadsheet is to reenter the information in the transposed format. Once you make a decision on how to organize the dimensions of a spreadsheet in these programs, changing your mind could require a lot of work.

Below are some guidelines of style:

- *As a general rule*, because most spreadsheet programs have more rows than columns (*Lotus 1-2-3* has 8,192 rows and 256 columns), use rows for the dimension that is more likely to expand. For example, in an inventory spreadsheet, use rows to hold the inventory items, and columns to hold details like inventory number, description, unit price, and stock count. This layout enables the spreadsheet to hold thousands of inventory items.

- *For a spreadsheet that is not expected to grow in size*, use rows for the larger of the two dimensions. That is, the block diagram of the spreadsheet should be in the shape of a vertical block, not a horizontal block. This takes advantage of spreadsheet program design, which allows easy scrolling and vertical printing. For example, if you have a spreadsheet table that takes up 50 cells in one dimension and 20 cells in the other dimension, make the shape of the spreadsheet vertical (50 rows by 20 columns) and not horizontal (20 rows by 50 columns).

- *For financial spreadsheets*, convention dictates that the separate financial items (such as expense categories) form the rows, and the time periods form the columns. Where the financial data is all from one time period, with information about several departments, it is good form to use columns for departments, and rows for the names of separate accounts.

- *Where one set of labels is long*, use rows for the longer labels (all else being equal). Column headings are best kept within the width of the column (which is normally set to the number of spaces required by the data in the column), and therefore cannot contain a large number of characters. Row labels, on the other hand, can be as long as desired, since the width of the column containing the labels can be tailored to fit the longest label.

- *For spreadsheets database applications* (see Chapter 11), the rows *must* be used for individual records, and the columns *must* be used for the data fields, because all database functions and commands require this structure.

3.2   MULTIPLE BLOCK DESIGN

Once a spreadsheet requires more than the basic layout of the single block described in Section 3.1, the recommended blocks are as follows.

Documentation Block

The documentation block contains information *about* the spreadsheet and does not include actual data. Typically, the spreadsheet developer would use this range of cells to enter a title for the spreadsheet, its filename, the identity of the developer, and the date of last revision. This information would be standardized and considered mandatory in many firms. Additional documentation might include information about the layout and working of the spreadsheet, location of named ranges, lists of macros and their purposes, and so on. (See Section 4.1 for more detail on this block.)

Input Block

The input block contains values that are used in formulas, and which are likely to change from time to time (such as the interest rate, or a sales markup). The formulas that use these values simply refer to the cell address in this block where the required input data are located.

There are several reasons for placing input data here rather than embedding them in formulas elsewhere on the spreadsheet. For clarity, because it is easier when doing what-if analysis or forecasting; for consistency, because the user can expect to find the input data always collected into a single featured block on any spreadsheet; and for accuracy, because the user need change only one cell (the input variable) instead of having to modify any formulas that used that value.

More advanced applications of this block are the input screen or dialog box. (See Section 4.2 for more detail on this block.)

Calculation Block

The calculation block is usually the main working block of the spreadsheet, includes formulas and fixed data. This block may be partitioned into several smaller blocks, whose functions will depend on the specific purpose of the spreadsheet. (See Section 4.3 for more detail.)

Output Block

The output block features the results, or output, of the calculations. It need not be placed at the "bottom line" of the spreadsheet, and may often be better located closer to the input block, so that the user can immediately see the results of changing input variables. (See Section 4.4 for more detail on this block.) The way the spreadsheet developer lays out these blocks is often of critical importance to the effective working of the spreadsheet.

Example.
Figures 3–1 and 3–2 provide examples of multiple block design. The figures show a cash budget spreadsheet for a small business, La Jolla Tools Rental. Figure 3–1*a* is the initial pencil and paper layout plan for the blocks. Figure 3–1*b* is the next step in detailing the layout, using columns and rows on paper. Figure 3–2 is the actual spreadsheet, including a simple title (A1), an input block (A3..C8), and a calculation block (A10..E45) that incorporates a summary of financing needs (A36..E45). For the purpose of this illustration, we have abbreviated the "documentation block" to a one-line title in cell A1; a fuller documentation block will be shown in Chapter 4. Note that a cash budget usually has categories of cash flows as one dimension, and time (quarters in this case) as

Figure 3-1*a*   Initial Block Design for Cash Budget Spreadsheet.

Title
Input data
Calculations
Output

FIGURE 3–1*b*   Detailed Block Design for Cash Budget Spreadsheet

A	B	C	D	E
Documentation - Title				
Input block ——— items ———		—— data ——		
Calculation block				
—— items ——	Q1	Q2	Q3	Q4
Output block – Financing	Q1	Q2	Q3	Q4
Borrowing				
Repayment				
Cash balance				
Line of credit				

FIGURE 3–2 Cash Budget Spreadsheet

	A	B	C	D	E
1	Cash Budget Spreadsheet				
2					
3	Input Data:				
4	Minimum cash balance desired:		$15,000		
5	Interest rate for line of credit:		10.00%		
6	Interest rate for bank balance:		5.00%		
7	Income tax rate:		25.00%		
8	Beginning loan balance (Qtr 1):		$1,000		
9					
10			La Jolla Tools Rental		
11			Cash Budget, 1990		
12			Quarters		
13					
14		1	2	3	4
15					
16	Cash balance, beginning	$10,000	$15,000	$15,000	$15,000
17	Receipts from customers	125,000	150,000	152,000	125,000
18	Interest income	0	570	725	0
19		--------	--------	--------	-------
20	Total available	135,000	165,000	167,000	140,000
21		--------	--------	--------	-------
22	Less disbursements:				
23	Payroll	100,000	100,000	100,000	100,000
24	Income tax	25,000	25,000	25,000	25,000
25	Rent	8,000	9,000	9,000	9,000
26	Interest expense	(1,545)	(405)	0	(186)
27	Other expenses	3,000	5,000	3,500	3,500
28		--------	--------	--------	-------
29	Total disbursements	134,455	138,595	137,500	137,314
30					
31	Min. cash bal. desired	15,000	15,000	15,000	15,000
32		--------	--------	--------	-------
33	Total cash needed	149,455	153,595	152,500	152,314
34	Excess (deficiency)	(14,455)	11,405	14,500	(12,314)
35		========	========	========	========
36	Financing:				
37	Borrowing(at begin)	14,455	0	0	12,314
38	Repayment(at end)	0	(11,405)	(14,500)	0
39		--------	--------	--------	-------
40	Total financing effect	14,455	(11,405)	(14,500)	12,314
41		--------	--------	--------	-------
42	Cash balance, end	15,000	15,000	15,000	15,000
43		========	========	========	========
44					
45	Line of credit (at end)	$15,455	$4,050	($10,450)	$1,863

FIGURE 3–3 Revised Block Design for Cash Budget Spreadsheet

Title
Input data
Output
Calculations

the other dimension. The correct style was a vertical layout with categories in the rows and time across the columns.

An alternative layout would have been to take the Financing block (A36..E45) and move it to immediately below the input block (A10). This would have the advantage of presenting the input data and output results on the same screen, saving the user the trouble of scrolling to the bottom line to see the results of changes made in the input data. The improved block layout is shown in Figure 3–3.

3.3 SAMPLE BLOCK DESIGNS

This section provides some samples of block designs for common financial spreadsheets, using the block design idea. To indicate the flexibility of this planning method, we have adapted the names and contents of the blocks to fit the purposes of each spreadsheet. The block design is by no means restricted to a company financial spreadsheet; it could work just as well for a household budget, a retail store inventory, a diet counter, or a a set of baseball league results.

Financial statements. Figure 3–4 is the block design for a worksheet that presents the commonly used financial statements. The documentation block can be as simple as the name of the business, the time periods that the statements cover, and the preparation date of the financial statements. Since this spreadsheet is not designed for what-if analysis (see Section 2.3), there is no input data block. The calculation block is made up of three parts, one for the balance sheet, one for the income statement, and one for the statement of retained earnings. In this model, the output is integrated in the calculation block, since every value calculated is of interest to the business operator.

FIGURE 3–4 Block Design for Financial Statements

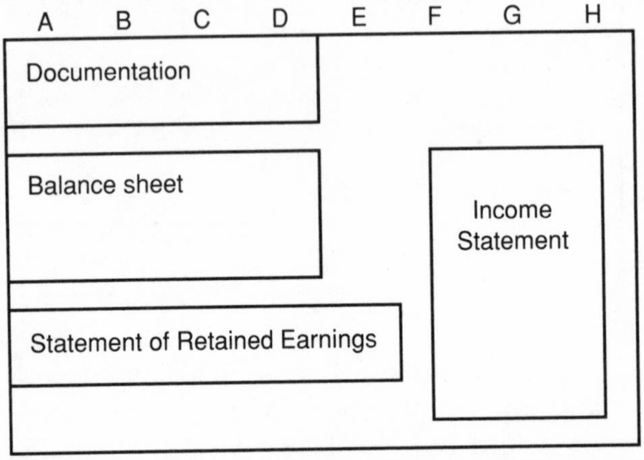

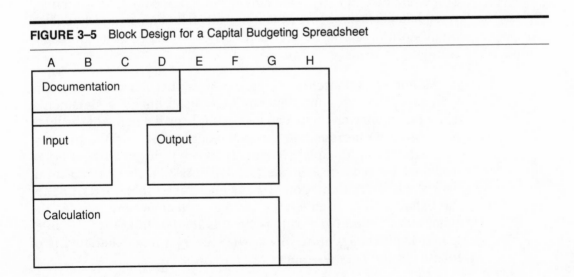

Capital budgeting spreadsheet. Figure 3–5 shows a four-block design, for a capital budgeting spreadsheet. The documentation block would include the purpose of the spreadsheet and how it is to be used. The input data block would contain the various assumptions used in the spreadsheet, and the input variables, such as cost of capital, initial investment cost, and cash inflows and outflows. The output block would contain the key results from the calculation block, and would provide the decision maker with a

FIGURE 3–5 Block Design for a Capital Budgeting Spreadsheet

FIGURE 3-6 Block Design for a Cash Purchase vs. Loan Analysis

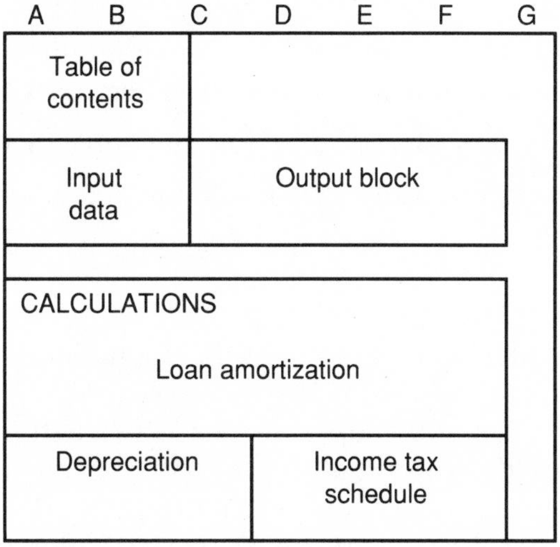

capsule view of the information needed for budget decisions. The output block is placed next to the input block so that the manager can change the input data and assumptions, and see the resulting output directly on-screen without having to browse the rest of the spreadsheet. The calculation block would contain the schedule that calculates the various measures used in capital budget decisions, such as calculated payback periods, net present values, and internal rates of return.

Financial analysis spreadsheet. There are many forms of financial analysis spreadsheets. A common one is a spreadsheet designed for comparing the purchase versus loan decision. Figure 3-6 shows a typical block design for this calculation. The documentation block can be quite brief, simply stating the purpose of the spreadsheet, and might include a "map" of the various parts of the model. The input block would contain the assumptions and the input variables, such as interest rate, the initial purchase price, the term of the loan, the income tax rate, the depreciation rate, and the salvage value. The output block would display the results obtained in the calculation block, and would summarize the calculations, comparing the purchase option against the loan alternative, in net present values. The calculation block would include schedules for loan amortization, depreciation, and income tax effect.

3.4 ADVANCED BLOCK DESIGN

A block design for more advanced spreadsheets could also include

- *Detailed documentation* such as programming comments, or "how to" instructions for the user (see Section 4.1).

- *Input screens and dialog boxes* for data entry (Section 4.2).

- *Macros* to automate repetitive tasks (Section 4.5 and Chapter 9).

- *Data tables* for lookup functions (Sections 8.6 and 8.7).

- *Criterion blocks* for database operations (Chapter 11).

The indicated references present style recommendations for these features.

The new generation of spreadsheets (such as *Lotus-1-2-3* Release 3) provides the capability of using a third dimension for spreadsheet management. The basic concept of *3-D spreadsheets* is that of a stack of spreadsheets: they may or may not be displayed in a three-dimensional visual format, and there are several variants on how the user links and arranges the spreadsheets. For instance, a monthly cash budget for the next 12 months for the entire company with details on 10 departments has a three-dimensional structure—cash flows, months, and departments. One design is to use rows for the cash flow items, columns for months (as in Figure 3–2), and the third dimension for departments. Each department occupies a two-dimensional spreadsheet, and the spreadsheets for all departments together form a complete three-dimensional model. (The design of three-dimensional spreadsheets is explained in more detail in Chapter 10.)

CHAPTER FOUR

Inside the Spreadsheet Blocks

The following sections provide additional guidelines for the content of the main parts of the spreadsheet in Chapter 3:

4.1 Documentation block (including program documentation)
4.2 Input block (including input screens and dialog boxes)
4.3 Calculation block
4.4 Output block
4.5 Macro block

Most of the style guidelines in this chapter apply to any kind of spreadsheet, whether it is organized in blocks, is loosely structured, or is freeform. The arrangement of the chapter into these topics is intended to assist readers in finding the ideas that most interest them.

4.1 DOCUMENTATION BLOCK

Even in spreadsheets designed for the developer's own use, it is a good practice to include *basic documentation* to identify

Title of spreadsheet
Filename
Date prepared
Date of last revision
Developer
User(s)

Other basic details that can be helpful to old and new users alike are

> Purpose of the spreadsheet
> Date and time printed

The best place for documentation is the top left corner of the spreadsheet, where the information is immediately readable by the user when the spreadsheet is loaded. Readability is further improved if the same information is presented in a consistent style on every spreadsheet.

Larger or complex spreadsheets often require more detailed *program documentation* about the design of the spreadsheet, its various parts, and how key features of the spreadsheet are set up to work for the user. This program documentation may include details about

> Names and locations of blocks of data
> Assumptions
> Named ranges
> Method of input
> Location of output
> Special formulas
> Special use of functions
> (Intentional) circular references
> Location and operation of macros
> Method of cell noting
> Operating procedures
> Cautions and limitations for use

The following documentation items merit attention.

Title. Give every spreadsheet a clearly descriptive title. A short form can be put in cell A1 for quick reference, and some thought should be given to the content and style of the main title that will appear centered over the data table. This title should inform the user, as directly and concisely as possible, of the content and purpose of the spreadsheet. Avoid long and possibly confusing titles by splitting them into a title and subtitle. All dates in a title should be explicit and must be carefully checked; take particular care if updating an old spreadsheet or working with a template.

Filename. The maximum number of characters permitted in a filename depends on the operating system. For example, MS-DOS,

PC-DOS, and OS/2 permit only a maximum of eight characters in a filename. The operating system used by the Apple Macintosh, however, permits a maximum of 32 characters. Operating systems used in minicomputers also permit filenames longer than eight characters.

The filename for a spreadsheet should carry as much meaning as possible, associating the name of the file with its content. A locally developed naming style can be of great value and reduce the risk of confusion and duplication within a work group.

Example.

A standard filename style was designed by a work group that handled multiple projects. They used *Lotus 1-2-3* Release 2.01 and the PC-DOS operating system. The rules of style were as follows.

1. Spreadsheet files must have exactly eight characters plus the three-character extension .WK1.
2. The first two characters of the filename are the firm's two-letter project code, such as BD for the Beaver Dam Project.
3. The third and fourth characters of the filename match the phase number of the project. Put a 0 in front of a single digit, such as 01 for phase 1, and 10 for phase 10.
4. The last four characters of the filename are the two-character staff ID assigned to each member of the project team and the sequential number of the spreadsheets developed by that member. Thus, JL03 is for John Lum's third spreadsheet, and BP06 for Bonita Perez's sixth.
5. The only acceptable extension is .WK1 until the upgrade to Release 3 is fully implemented and staff advised.

Sample Filenames:

BD01JL03.WK1   Beaver Dam Project, Phase 1, John Lum, spreadsheet #3

OL10BP06.WK1   Ozone Layer Project, Phase 10, Bonita Perez, spreadsheet #6

Developer. The developer of the spreadsheet should be identified so that other users can establish contact and find out additional information on data, the rationale for formulas, the source and currency of the data, and so on. In some work groups, only the developer of the spreadsheet may be allowed to change it, and a password locking system may be set up for this purpose.

Passwords, of course, should never be entered on the spreadsheet!

User(s).   It may be helpful to identify the intended users of a spreadsheet. Sometimes, when an old spreadsheet is found on the files, it can be quite a puzzle to discover its purpose and once-intended use. Identifying the developer and user may help solve the puzzle.

Date and time.   For spreadsheets that are subject to many changes and updates, it is very important to see not only the date of the original version, but also the date of the latest revision. A variant of this style is to insert a "date and time stamp" in the documentation block, if the spreadsheet program provides such a function. If there is no built-in function, enter the date and time stamp as a text label. For example, the integer portion of the @NOW function in *Lotus 1-2-3* provides the current system date; the decimal portion provides the hours and minutes. Using a date and time stamp function in a spreadsheet, rather than entering it as text, ensures that each time the spreadsheet is loaded or printed, the date and time will be current.

If the spreadsheet program permits date and time stamps to be included in the header or footer of a printed page, you may adopt the style of specifying the date and time stamp in the print option rather than in the documentation block. For example, specifying an "at" sign (@) in the header or footer in the */Print* command in *Lotus 1-2-3* Release 2.01 results in a date and time stamp on every printed page.

Program documentation.   Many spreadsheets should contain information beyond the basic matters of identification. We have referred to these items as program documentation, and listed typical items at the beginning of this chapter. In general, program documentation should include any information that is required for the maintenance and modification of the spreadsheet.

Example.

Figure 4–1 shows a detailed documentation block for a cash flow projection spreadsheet. Cell A1 contains a short form of the title for immediate identification. The short title is placed in this cell (rather than centered) because the spreadsheet program in use will display the contents of cell A1 in the file listing. The filename is placed in D1. Cells B2 and B3 are formatted to this firm's standard house style for dates. The developer and user of the spreadsheet are not the same, and are therefore shown. Date and time of

FIGURE 4–1   Detailed Documentation

	A	B	C	D	E
1	Cash flow projection - Q2, 1989			File:	CASHPROJ.WK1
2	Date prepared:	2/12/90			
3	Date last revised:	2/18/90			
4	Developer:	F. Miller			
5	User:	C. Imetz			
6	Purpose:	Cash flow planning			
7	Date printed:	2/18/90			
8	Time printed:	2:15 pm			
9					
10	Assumption:				
11	Interest rate:	12.00%			
12					
13	Limitations:				
14	(a) Interest cost for month based on ending loan balance.				
15	(b) Loan repayment in any month must be manually entered.				
16					
17	---				
18		Burnaby Highway Motel			
19		Cash Flow Projection			
20		For the Quarter to 30-Jun-90			
21					

printing are another aspect of house style used in this firm. The next block of information (A10..A15) provides documentation of the assumptions and limitations of the spreadsheet, and incorporates cell B11 as a location for input of the variable interest rate. Row 17 acts as a divider between documentation and the actual title (B18..B20) of the main calculation block of the spreadsheet.

Figure 4–2 shows another part of the same spreadsheet. Cell range H1..O7 is basically another part of the documentation block, used to record information about the workings of this spreadsheet model, in this case circular references and named ranges. (See also Chapter 5.)

FIGURE 4–2   Program Documentation

	H	I	J	K	L	M	N
1	Program documentation:						
2							
3	(a) Circular references in rows 24, 29, and 42.						
4	(b) Named ranges and their meaning:						
5		Name	Cell	Meaning			
6		LOANIN	C10	Interest rate for loans			
7		INVESTIN	C11	Interest rate for investments			

FIGURE 4–3 Simple Input Screen

	A	B	C	D	E	F
1						
2	Enter the following information about the loan:					
3						
4			--			
5			Principal...................$10,000.00			
6			Interest rate.............. 10.00%			
7			Term (months).............. 2			
8			Compounding periods/year... 12			
9			Status at payment period... 9			
10						
11			--			
12						
13						
14						

4.2 INPUT BLOCK

In Chapter 3, Section 3.2, we explained the merits of grouping input data in a block separate from the formulas since, ideally, formulas should not contain variable data, but should incorporate cell addresses where those data are to be input and stored. This section outlines two styles of formalizing the input of those variable data: input screens and dialog boxes.

Input Screens for Data Entry

A simple way to standardize data input into a spreadsheet is to design an input screen. An input screen can be as simple as a range of cells separated from the main calculation block and reserved for data entry by the user.

Example.

In Figure 4–3, the input screen in cells A2..F11 is placed in a separate cell range by itself so that it does not share any space with the output block or the calculation block on the same screen. That is, the input area takes up all 20 rows of a screen. An input screen can also be more detailed and provide the user with questions. Figure 4–4 shows a more detailed input screen design which enables the user to enter information about personal retirement needs. The rest of the spreadsheet then provides an analysis of the possible outcomes of the retirement investment plan.

FIGURE 4–4   A More Detailed Input Screen

```
         A       B       C       D       E       F         G
 1  Retirement planning spreadsheet
 2
 3  Date:     14-Apr-90
 4
 5  Provide the following information about your retirement needs:
 6
 7     1. The amount of principal and interest presently
 8        in your retirement plan is ...................    $100,000
 9
10     2. You wish to retire at the age of: ...........         60
11
12     3. Your present age is .........................         45
13
14     4. Years you wish to receive retirement income:         15
15
16     5. The average annual contribution you will make is:
17                                    Alternative 1:      $5,000
18                                    Alternative 2:      $3,000
19                                    Alternative 3:      $1,000
20
21     6. The expected average annual difference between
22        interest earned and inflation will be:
23        (example: enter 12% as .12)     Best case:         6.00%
24                                        Most likely case:  8.00%
25                                        Worst case:       10.00%
26
27  ...................................................................
```

Guidelines for Input Screens

The following style guidelines are recommended for input screens.

- Set up the wording and layout of the input screen so that it closely matches that of any paper forms from which the data are transferred. Any time an operator has to rearrange data, there is an increased risk of error.

- If no forms have been used, lay out the input screen so that the order of entry matches the natural flow of information.

- The input cells should be preformatted so that the user can quickly spot entry errors. For example, a cell to contain a dollar amount should be preformatted to show the dollar sign, thousand commas, and decimal point.

- The unit or scale should also be clearly indicated. Where there may be ambiguity, provide clear instructions or display an example.

FIGURE 4–5 Dialog Box Using Excel

	A	B	C	D	E	F	G	H	I
	A16								
1	High Fashion Import/Export Inc.								
2		Part	Unit	Warehouse #1		Warehouse #2			
3	Item Name	Number	Cost	QuantityW1	ValueW1	QuantityW2	ValueW2		

```
Name:          [                    ]          Part No.  Format:
                                               Ladies'  =  1XXXX        [   Enter item   ]
                                               Mens'    =  2XXXX
Unit_cost:     [                    ]          Girls'   =  3XXXX
                                               Boys'    =  4XXXX
Quantity_1:    [                    ]                                   [    Cancel     ]

                                               Part_No.:
Quantity_2:    [                    ]          [                    ]
```

For Help on dialog settings, press F1

- Where possible, error checking should be performed during data input. Several methods of error checking can be employed. The simplest method is to place a formula adjacent to each input data cell to check data validity. (This technique and others are described in Chapter 7.)

Dialog Boxes and Data-Entry Forms

With *Microsoft Excel*, you can design custom dialog boxes to prompt for data input. Dialog boxes, like data input screens, should be designed to closely match the paper input form or the physical flow of information. Figure 4–5 shows an input dialog box designed using *Excel*.

In *Lotus 1-2-3 Release 3*, data-entry forms can be designed by using macro commands. These forms are similar in function to Excel's dialog boxes. On-screen forms can be custom designed for users to enter data which is then copied by means of the macro and pasted into the actual database area.

The use of dialog boxes and data-entry forms can greatly simplify data input to databases.

4.3 CALCULATION BLOCK

The calculation block contains two kinds of cell contents: data that are unlikely to change and therefore inappropriate for inclusion in the input block, and spreadsheet formulas that perform calculations on the spreadsheet data. This section will set out guidelines for formula construction, including suggestions for improving the use of common spreadsheet functions, such as AVG, IF, and CHOOSE. (See also Chapter 8 for more detailed information on the use of the IF and CHOOSE functions.)

Guidelines for Formula Construction

Keep Formulas Simple. The most important rule for formula construction is to "keep it simple." By doing so, the spreadsheet will be less prone to error and easier to maintain.

Example.
The following two *Lotus 1-2-3* formulas yield identical results, but the second formula is unnecessarily complicated.

```
+A5+A7+A9+A10-A13
@SUM(A5,A7,A9..A10,-A13)
```

Example.
While parentheses may clarify the components of a formula, excessive use of parentheses can make the formula too complicated and virtually impossible to understand. For instance, the following two *Lotus 1-2-3* formulas yield identical results, but parentheses actually obscure the meaning of the second one.

```
(A3*A4+A5*1.4-A6*(100-A7/A8))/1.5-A9^(1/6)
(((A3*A4)+(A5*1.4)-(A6*(100-(A7/A8))))/1.5)-(A9^(1/6))
```

Balance the parentheses. When parentheses occur in a formula, use this simple rule of thumb to check that you have the correct number: Count the number of opening (right facing) parentheses and make sure this number matches the number of closing (left facing) parentheses. Unfortunately, the check does not guarantee that you have them in the right places!

Use functions to simplify. Spreadsheet programs provide a number of built-in functions. A function is a predetermined formula designed to perform a specific calculation or operation. Functions that are typically supplied with spreadsheet programs include the following:

Arithmetic	such as rounding and square roots
Calendar	such as subtracting dates to count days
Database	such as averaging a database field
Financial	such as investment and annuities
Logical	such as IF and CHOOSE
Statistical	such as means and standard deviations
Trigonometric	such as sines, cosines, and radians

Advanced programs may include other functions such as cell text, index, and advanced logical operations. The advantage of a function is that it makes formulas simpler, and easier to remember.

Example.

Three formulas are printed below. The first calculates the average value of a range of cells without using built-in functions, the second accomplishes the same task using two functions, and the third takes advantage of one function to accomplish the same results. The formula with the AVG function would be the preferred style for most spreadsheets because it is simpler, more readable, and easier to modify.

```
(D1+D2+D3+D4+D5+D6+D7+D8+D9+D10+D11+D12+D13+D14)/14
@SUM(D1..D14)/ @COUNT(D1..D14)
@AVG(D1..D14)
```

Become familiar with the list of functions that are available on your spreadsheet. It may be possible to use one to replace an otherwise complex formula or procedure.

Keep formulas short and concise.

The IF function is very common in spreadsheets. It requires three arguments to be specified, in the following form:

```
IF(logical expression,action if true,action if false)
```

Example.

The IF function is used to determine one of two possible alternative actions. To select from more than two alternatives, the IF function can be nested. However, if there are more than three or four choices, the nesting of one IF clause inside another, itself inside another, and so on, can become very complicated. For example,

FIGURE 4–6 Using Intermediate Calculations

	A	B	C	D	E	F	G
9	Net sales	$34,567			Commission	rate	table:
10	Commission payments:				Net sales	Base	Excess
11	Commission bracket	$30,000			$5,000	$60	1.60%
12	Base commission	$540			$7,500	$120	1.67%
13	Excess percent	1.76%			$12,000	$200	1.71%
14	Commission amount	$620			$17,500	$300	1.79%
15					$20,000	$357	1.80%
16					$30,000	$540	1.76%
17					$45,000	$790	1.74%
18					$55,000	$920	1.60%

the following *Lotus 1-2-3* formula returns one of seven possible values, depending on the content of cell A1.

```
@IF(A10=1,1.5,@IF(A10=2,1.75,@IF(A10=3,2.0,@IF(A10=4,
2.25,@IF(A10=5,2.5,@IF(A10=6,2.75,@ERR))))))
```

Although this use of the IF function is not incorrect, it renders the formula unclear, unreadable, and very difficult for anyone else to use or adapt. It would be better style to use the CHOOSE function that could achieve the same result.

```
@CHOOSE(A10-1,1.5,1.75,2.0,2.25,2.5,2.75)
```

In other words, check the value in cell A10 and take 1 from it; if the result is 0, display the value 1.5; if the result is 1, display the value 1.75 . . .(and so on). (See Chapter 8 for more information on the IF and CHOOSE functions.)

To reduce long formulas, use intermediate calculations.

Break a long formula into several steps, and display the intermediate calculation steps in clearly marked cells in the calculation block of the spreadsheet.

Example.

Figure 4–6 is part of a *Lotus 1-2-3* spreadsheet to calculate sales commissions for agents. It shows how to use intermediate calculations to break up and simplify a long formula.

The commission paid to an agent for any week is calculated from a commission rate table. To compute the commission, the spreadsheet looks up each agent's net sales for the week to determine the base amount. Any sales in excess of the base earns additional commission at a prescribed rate. Thus, if net sales are $34,567, this amount falls between the net sales brackets of $30,000 and $45,000 in the commission rate table. The base amount of commission is $540; the excess sales over $30,000 earn commission at the rate of 1.76 percent. Thus, the total amount of commission is the base amount of $540, plus a further 1.76 percent of $4,567, that is, $80. The resulting total commission is $620.

It would take a rather complex formula to put this computation into one cell. Using the information supplied, and recruiting the LOOKUP function (which is the most appropriate for looking up values in a reference table), this single formula for total commission amount would be entered into the output block of Figure 4–6.

```
@VLOOKUP(B9,E11..G18,1)+@VLOOKUP(B9,E11..G18,2)*
    (B9-@VLOOKUP(B9,E11..G18,0)
```

The developer of this spreadsheet, however, decided to use the alternative style of breaking the computation into steps. Accordingly, in Figure 4–6, instead of using the single complex formula, she entered the following three formulas in cells B11, B12, and B13, yielding the solution in cell B14.

```
B11:    @VLOOKUP(B9,E11..G18,0)
B12:    @VLOOKUP(B9,E11..G18,1)
B13:    @VLOOKUP(B9,E11..G18,2)
B14:    +B12+(B9-B11)*B13
```

Notice also in Figure 4–6 that the developer grouped the intermediate calculations into a small range (B11..B13), thereby improving the readability of the spreadsheet. One limitation of the intermediate calculation style, however, is that it may prove distracting or interruptive to the reader. This is a judgement call.

4.4 OUTPUT BLOCK

Sometimes the results of calculations are scattered across a spreadsheet. Even if results are all arranged in an orderly and consistent style at the bottom of columns, readability will often be improved if the data are summarized in a separate output block on the spreadsheet.

Example.

Figure 4–7 shows a loan amortization spreadsheet with three blocks, one for input, one for calculations, and one for output. Notice that the results appear right next to the input block so that the user does not need to see the calculation block, unless necessary. For our purposes, only the first 12 months of the calculation block are shown in Figure 4–7.

FIGURE 4–7   Amortization Spreadsheet with Three Blocks

```
     A      B        C        D        E       F       G        H
 1  Loan Amortization
 2
 3  Input data:                          |Output:
 4  -------------------------------------|-------------------------------------
 5  Principal.................$10,000.00 |Total number of payments..      24
 6  Interest rate..............  10.00%  |Monthly payment amount....  $461.45
 7  Term (months)..............      2   |At payment period    9
 8  Compounding periods/year...     12   |  Interest component......   $57.38
 9  Status at payment period...      9   |  Principal component.....  $404.07
10                                       |  Principal balance.......$6,481.29
11  ------------------------------------------------------------------------
12  Calculations:
13
14           Payment  Interest  Principal  Principal
15  Period   Amount   Component Component   Balance
16  ...........................................
17        1  $461.45   $83.33    $378.12   $9,621.88
18        2   461.45    80.18     381.27    9240.62
19        3   461.45    77.01     384.44    8856.17
20        4   461.45    73.80     387.65    8468.53
21        5   461.45    70.57     390.88    8077.65
22        6   461.45    67.31     394.14    7683.51
23        7   461.45    64.03     397.42    7286.09
24        8   461.45    60.72     400.73    6885.36
25        9   461.45    57.38     404.07    6481.29
26       10   461.45    54.01     407.44    6073.85
27       11   461.45    50.62     410.83    5663.02
28       12   461.45    47.19     414.26    5248.76
```

The user enters variable data in cells D5 to D9, and the required information appears in the output block (H5..H10). This layout permits the user to obtain the necessary information at a glance without having to browse through pages of the spreadsheet. For instance, without this design, the user seeking information about Period 60 would have to search through several pages of the detailed loan amortization schedule to obtain this information.

A three-dimensional spreadsheet would provide an even neater solution to the design problem of deriving results from multiple blocks of data and presenting those results in succinct form to the reader (see also Chapter 10).

4.5   MACRO BLOCKS

Macros are sometimes added to streamline the procedures of more advanced spreadsheets. This section will suggest some points of style for their placement on the spreadsheet (See also Chapter 9).

FIGURE 4–8   Adding a Macro Block

```
        A       B        C         D          E      F     G       H        I
 1   Loan Amortization
 2
 3   Input data:                          |Output:
 4   ------------------------------------ |------------------------------------
 5   Principal.................$10,000.00 |Total number of payments..     24
 6   Interest rate..............  10.00%  |Monthly payment amount....  $461.45
 7   Term (months)..............    2     |At payment period   9
 8   Compounding periods/year...   12     |  Interest component......   $57.38
 9   Status at payment period:..    9     |  Principal component.....  $404.07
10                                        |  Principal balance.......$6,481.29
11   ---------------------------------------------------------------------------
12   Calculations:                                 Macros:
13                                                 The \P macro prints the input data
14            Payment Interest Principal Principal    and output summary only:
15   Period   Amount  Component Component Balance   \P   {CALC}     Recalculates
16           ................................            /PPCA      Clears all settings
17       1   $461.45   $83.33   $378.12  $9,621.88       RA1.H13~   Sets output range
18       2    461.45    80.18    381.27   9240.62        AS\015~Q   Sets compressed mode
19       3    461.45    77.01    384.44   8856.1         GPQ        Prints and quits
20       4    461.45    73.80    387.65   8468.53
21       5    461.45    70.57    390.88   8077.65   The \S macro prints the loan
22       6    461.45    67.31    394.14   7683.51      amortization table:
23       7    461.45    64.03    397.42   7286.09   \S   {CALC}
24       8    461.45    60.72    400.73   6885.36        /PPCA      Clears all settings
25       9    461.45    57.38    404.07   6481.29        RA14.E28~  Sets output range
26      10    461.45    54.01    407.44   6073.85        AGPQ       Prints and quits
27      11    461.45    50.62    410.83   5663.02
28      12    461.45    47.19    414.26   5248.76
```

Example.

If a developer wanted to add a macro to the spreadsheet in Figure 4–7, the spreadsheet could be structured along the lines of Figure 4–8. The macro block comprises cells F12 to H26. This part of the spreadsheet was chosen because it would not be affected by changes elsewhere in the spreadsheet. Two macros are included, each headed by a brief commentary and a line-by-line annotation.

Location of Macros

There is no firm style among spreadsheet users as to the best location for macros. The most common choices are

- In the far right columns of the spreadsheet, as far away from the spreadsheet data and calculation blocks as possible.

- To the right of the calculation block.

- Below the data variables and calculation blocks.
- In the top left corner following the documentation.

Figure 4–8 illustrates one style. To some extent, the best location depends on the makeup of the rest of the spreadsheet. The following rules may help choose the most suitable location for macros.

1. Place macros in a location where they are unlikely to be affected by the insertion or deletion of rows and columns.

   Example.

   Do not place macros to the right of the formula block if there is a possibility of inserting or deleting rows in the formula block. In most spreadsheet programs, you use a blank cell to signal the end of a macro. Therefore, the accidental insertion of a blank row in the middle of a macro would result in the macro terminating execution prematurely. In some spreadsheet programs, the macros are not affected by blank cells, but in any case, macros with blank cells can present other problems, and should generally be avoided.

   Note that in Figure 4–8, the number of rows in the calculation block are fixed and sequential: there is little probability that an extra row would be inserted which might interfere with the macro. To further reduce such a risk, cell protection could be applied (see Section 6.5).

2. Place macros in a location where they will not interfere with the operation of the spreadsheet.

   Example.

   Many spreadsheets designed for database applications require data to be appended to the bottom of the database block. In such cases, macros should not be placed below the database block.

3. Place macros in a location where they are unlikely to interfere with the printing of the spreadsheet. For instance, do not place macros in the midst of calculations that may need to be printed out for analysis and confirmation.

4. Document the macros with comment lines. Information on the location, purpose, and cautions regarding macros should also appear in the documentation block (see Section 4.1 of this chapter).

CHAPTER FIVE

Cell Addresses and Referencing

This chapter presents style guidelines for using cell addresses and the process of cell referencing. It is divided into the following sections:

5.1   Cell addresses and cell references
5.2   Relative cell references
5.3   Absolute cell references
5.4   Mixed cell references
5.5   Guidelines for relative, absolute, and mixed references
5.6   Circular references and iteration
5.7   Guidelines for iteration
5.8   Locating unwanted circular references
5.9   Guidelines for circular references
5.10 Named ranges
5.11 Guidelines for named ranges

NOTE: In the remaining chapters of this manual, the illustrative spreadsheets have been simplified in various ways for the purposes of publication. Thus, documentation blocks are typically not shown, and the structure of the spreadsheet is modified to fit within a single page of the manual.

5.1   CELL ADDRESSES AND CELL REFERENCES

The *address* of a cell consists of its respective column letter and row number, taken from the borders of the spreadsheet. All spreadsheet programs display the address of the active cell on-screen and feature a highlighted cursor that can be instructed to move to specific cell addresses.

Formulas in a spreadsheet commonly include the addresses of cells that store data needed to calculate the formulas. The addresses may be entered into the formulas from the keyboard, or there may be a system of *pointing* to cells with the cursor and routinely capturing their addresses this way.

Cells that are *referenced* by formulas in this way are usually to be found in the same spreadsheet. However, if the spreadsheet program can *link* two or more spreadsheets, the formulas may refer to cells in other spreadsheets. (See Chapter 10 for more on linked, multiple, and 3-D spreadsheets.)

Almost all spreadsheet programs accept the following types of cell reference:

- relative cell references

- absolute cell references

- mixed cell references

- circular references

5.2 RELATIVE CELL REFERENCES

Relative cell reference is the default setting for all spreadsheet programs. If you have a formula in cell B6 that reads +A4+A5, you will understand this as "add A4 and A5 and put the result in B6," but the spreadsheet actually remembers the instruction as "add together the values in the two cells immediately above this one and one column to the left, then put the value in this cell." In other words, it recognizes and stores cell values on the basis of their *relative* locations.

The main significance of all this is revealed when a formula or function is copied to a different location on the spreadsheet. Unless you instruct otherwise (by using an absolute reference), the formula will adjust the cell addresses relative to the new location. So if you copy B6 to D6, that same formula will change to +C4+C5.

Example.

Say that cell D12 contains a formula that references cell C12, converting C12 from miles to kilometers.

+C12*1.6093

If the formula is part of a table where column C contains distance measured in miles, and you copy the formula to the next row down (cell D13), the cell address is automatically adjusted to reflect its new location, and the formula becomes

```
+C13*1.6093
```

Similarly, if you copied the same formula to a cell another four rows down, it would read

```
+C17*1.6093
```

In other words, the spreadsheet recognizes that the formula has moved and adjusts all cell references relative to the new location. Most of the time, this is very convenient and exactly what the spreadsheet developer wants.

Relative reference works the same way for copying to the left or right. If the original formula is copied two columns to the right, the formula would be changed to

```
+E12*1.6093
```

Several cell references in one formula.   If there is more than one relative cell reference in a formula, all of the references are changed as the formula is copied to other locations.

Moving cells.   Most spreadsheet programs provide a means to move a formula from one cell to another, without relative referencing taking effect. If cell D12 has the formula +C12*1.6093 and is *moved* (not copied) to cell D13, the resultant formula in cell D13 is still +C12*1.6093. It is therefore very important to make the distinction between copying a formula and moving a formula: the former adjusts the cell references in the formula, while the latter does not.

Inserting or deleting rows and columns.   All spreadsheet programs permit rows and columns to be inserted or deleted. Formulas containing cell references are automatically adjusted. Adjustment is essential to ensure that the insertion or deletion of rows or columns does not result in erroneous formulas.

To adjust or not adjust.   The automatic changing of cell references is called *formula adjustment*. In some programs, you may be given the option *not* to adjust when copying a cell formula from one cell to another. However, *absolute referencing* is an easier way to instruct the spreadsheet not to adjust (see Section 5.3).

FIGURE 5–1   Use of Relative Cell Reference

	A	B	C	D	E
5					
6		Oficina Inc.			
7		Inventory Control Summary			
8					
9		Stock	Unit		
10	Product	Ident.	Cost	Quant.	Value
11	---				
12	Dallas chair	CHD 109	57.50	15	862.50
13	Bunk bed	BBD 317	350.00	8	2,800.00
14	Cabinet 18x20x34"	CAB 101	126.00	10	1,260.00
15	Cabinet 18x20x54"	CAB 102	187.50	11	2,062.50
16	Conference chair	CHC 208	37.00	24	888.00
17	Office desk 48x20"	DKO 121	234.75	9	2,112.75
18	Swivel chair	CHS 215	89.25	12	1,071.00
19	Typewriter table	TBT 110	115.00	16	1,840.00

Example.

Figure 5–1, an inventory control summary for a furniture store, shows a typical use of relative reference in cell formulas. Note that, to simplify the example, we have not included the documentation part of the spreadsheet. Cells E12:E19 are the only cells containing formulas. The formula in cell E12 (inventory value for Dallas chairs) is +C12*D12 representing unit cost multiplied by quantity on hand. When copied from cell E12 to cell E13, the spreadsheet program automatically adjusts the formula to +C13*D13.

5.3   ABSOLUTE CELL REFERENCES

Sometimes you want the cell reference in a formula to stay the same—that is, be the *absolute* same. You do not want it to change when the formula is copied anywhere else in the spreadsheet.

The standard way to indicate an absolute cell reference is the dollar sign ($). This use of the dollar sign is just a standard convention adopted by spreadsheet programs; in this form it does not have anything to do with currency. Thus, the reference $D$5 means the value of cell D5. Wherever this formula is copied in the spreadsheet, this absolute reference will remain unchanged. Note that, in this example, the dollar sign is entered before the column letter, and before the row number. (A variation of this rule, the mixed cell reference, is explained in Section 5.4.)

FIGURE 5–2 Use of Absolute Cell Reference

```
       A       B        C         D          E
5    Exchange rate (Cdn to US):      1.21
6
7
8
9              Otus Development Canada Corporation
10                     Income statement
11               For the quarter ended March 31, 1990
12
13                                Cdn funds    US funds
14
15   Sales                        2,400,000   1,983,471
16   Less: Cost of goods sold       800,000     661,157
17                               ------------------------
18   Gross margin                 1,600,000   1,322,314
19
20   Expenses
21      Selling expense             250,000     206,612
22      Office rent                 300,000     247,934
23      Salaries                    450,000     371,901
24      Advertising and promotions  150,000     123,967
25      Administrative expenses      11,000       9,091
26                               ------------------------
27       Total expenses          1,161,000     959,504
28                               ------------------------
29   Net income                     439,000     362,810
30                               ========================
```

Example.

Figure 5–2 shows how absolute cell references are used in formulas. The value in cell E15 is calculated from the formula +D15/$D$5 which converts sales revenue from Canadian funds to U.S. funds. The formula was first entered manually in cell E15. The developer of this spreadsheet (who used good style) did not want the divisor in this formula to change; the reference $D$5 meant "use the value that has been entered in cell D5." But it was necessary to allow the numerator (top part) of the fraction to change as the formula was copied to the cells below.

Thus, when the formula was copied to cell E16, the formula became +D16/$D$5. In fact, the formula could be copied to any cell, and the reference to cell D5 would always remain unchanged.

Deleting or Inserting Rows and Columns

An absolute cell reference is changed by the spreadsheet program if rows or columns are deleted or inserted, *and* these modifications result in a change in the physical location of the referenced cell.

Example.

Suppose that, in an income statement (Figure 5–2), you decide to add another item of documentation above A5 ("Exchange rate") and insert a row above row 5. This modification will affect the physical location of cell D5, moving it down to cell D6. Consequently, the spreadsheet program will recognize the absolute reference in any formulas referencing the old cell D5 and will automatically adjust the absolute references to that cell to $D$6 in each formula.

The table in Figure 5–2 was used by a company that needed to show its statements in U.S. and Canadian funds. The use of absolute cell reference makes it easy to build the income statement; the only formula that needs to be manually entered for the U.S. funds column is the one in cell E15. This formula is then copied to the rest of the cells in the column. When the exchange rate changes, it is only necessary to enter the new rate in cell D5; the spreadsheet will automatically recalculate the U.S. funds column to reflect the new rate.

5.4 MIXED CELL REFERENCES

A cell address or reference always comprises two parts—a column letter (or letters) and a row number. Thus, the *relative* cell reference C12 refers to the cell in column C, row 12. The *absolute* cell reference $C$12 fixes both parts of the reference so that neither part will change if a formula is copied. A *mixed* cell reference has one part absolute (that is, fixed) and the other part relative (that is, adjustable).

For example, the mixed cell reference $C12 indicates that the column part of the reference is fixed at column C, but leaves the row reference of 12 relative. Similarly, the cell reference C$12 fixes the row reference to row 12. Most spreadsheet programs that support the use of absolute and mixed cell references provide a function key to facilitate the use of absolute and mixed cell reference without requiring the user to enter the dollar sign($). For example, *Lotus 1-2-3* uses the <**F4**> key to rotate through relative, absolute, and mixed cell reference while a formula is being constructed.

FIGURE 5–3 Mixed Cell Reference

	A	B	C	D	E	F	G
5							
6			Oficina Inc.				
7			Inventory List				
8							
9		Stock	Unit	Broadway	Store	Madison	Store
10	Product	Ident.	Cost	Quant.	Value	Quant.	Value
11	---						
12	Dallas chair	CHD 109	57.50	15	862.50	12	690.00
13	Bunk bed	BBD 317	350.00	8	2,800.00	11	3,850.00
14	Cabinet 18x20x34"	CAB 101	126.00	10	1,260.00	7	882.00
15	Cabinet 18x20x54"	CAB 102	187.50	11	2,062.50	15	2,812.50
16	Conference chair	CHC 208	37.00	24	888.00	30	1,110.00
17	Office desk 48x20"	DKO 121	234.75	9	2,112.75	8	1,878.00
18	Swivel chair	CHS 215	89.25	12	1,071.00	14	1,249.50
19	Typewriter table	TBT 110	115.00	16	1,840.00	22	2,530.00
20							

Example.

Figure 5–3 shows a spreadsheet for Oficina Inc., containing inventory information for the Broadway and Madison stores. The cells containing formulas are found in E12:E19 and G12:G19. Thus

> The formula in cell E12 is +$C12*D12.
> When copied to cell E13, it becomes +$C13*D13.
> When copied to cell G12, it becomes +$C12*F12.

The use of the mixed cell reference made setting up the formulas for the Madison store faster and more efficient by copying the formulas for the Broadway store.

5.5 GUIDELINES FOR RELATIVE, ABSOLUTE AND MIXED REFERENCES

Many spreadsheets require only relative cell references. For some spreadsheet models, however, absolute references are essential for accuracy. In other situations, the purpose of using an absolute or mixed reference may be to speed up formula building, save time, and reduce the risk of error.

The following guidelines will be useful.

- *Absolute cell reference* must be used in a formula if the reference must stay constant, wherever the formula is copied.

- *Mixed cell reference* should be used if the formula is to be copied to other rows and other columns, where reference to a certain row or column (rather than a specific cell) is to remain constant.

- *Relative cell reference* should be used in all other cases.

5.6 CIRCULAR REFERENCES AND ITERATION

Circular reference describes one of two situations.

1. The formula in a cell references the same cell in which the formula resides.
2. The formula in a cell depends on the calculated result of another cell, which in turn depends on the calculated result of the first cell.

In some cases, a circular cell reference is clearly an error. Situation 1 is always an error. Situation 2 may be an error, or may be necessary to properly solve a problem. If you are using a spreadsheet prepared by someone else (or perhaps are dusting off an old one of your own), it is particularly important to know whether a circular reference is accidental or intentional.

Most spreadsheet programs provide a visible warning whenever a circular reference is detected in a spreadsheet. For example, *Lotus 1-2-3* displays a "CIRC" indicator in one corner of the screen.

Example 1.

Suppose cell C15 contains the formula @SUM(C4..C15). This is the first type of circular reference and is always an error.

Example 2.

Figures 5–4*a* and 5–4*b* show a cash flow projection for October through December for Westcoast Import and Export. Figure 5–4*a* shows the spreadsheet, and Figure 5–4*b* shows underlying formulas for October. In cell B19, the formula for interest income for October is @IF(B34>0,$B$7*B34,0) if there is any cash excess for the month (cell B34). The amount of cash excess is calculated by subtracting total cash receipts from total cash disbursements. However, circular reasoning occurs because total cash receipts include interest income for the month. A similar circular reference exists for interest expense (see the formula in cell B29).

This particular cash flow projection model cannot easily be calculated without the use of circular reference. Note that the documentation portion of the spreadsheet indicates (in row 5) rows where circular reference has intentionally been used.

FIGURE 5–4a Circular Reference (Spreadsheet)

	A	B	C	D
5	Circular references used:	Rows 19, 29, and 32		
6	Assumptions:			
7	1. Expected monthly interest rate:	1.00%		
8	2. Interest income = cash excess * monthly interest rate			
9	3. Interest expense = cash shortage * monthly interest rate			
10				
11	---			
12		Westcoast Import and Export Inc.		
13		Cash flow projection		
14		For the period 10/1/90 to 12/31/90		
15				
16		Oct 90	Nov 90	Dec 90
17	Cash receipts:			
18	Accounts receivable collection	$104,800	$112,560	$113,967
19	Interest income	0	125	0
20	Other cash receipts	5,000	6,000	9,000
21		-------	-------	-------
22	Total cash receipts	109,800	118,685	122,967
23				
24	Cash disbursements:			
25	Wages & salaries	60,000	55,000	69,000
26	Rent	10,000	10,000	10,000
27	Selling expenses	17,010	17,223	17,438
28	Advertising	12,000	11,000	15,000
29	Interest expense	43	0	25
30	Other expenses	15,000	13,000	14,000
31		-------	-------	-------
32	Total cash disbursements	114,053	106,223	125,463
33		-------	-------	-------
34	Cash excess (shortage)	($4,253)	$12,462	($2,496)
35		===============================		

Iteration and Circular Reference

Spreadsheet programs resolve circular reference by *iteration*. Iteration in a spreadsheet is the repetition of calculations until the values in formulas stop changing. If a spreadsheet contains a circular reference, most spreadsheet programs will automatically perform iterations of the calculations and recalculations until the formulas are resolved. In the iteration process, the new values in the formulas are compared with the old values each time a circular reference is recalculated. If the difference (called *delta*) between the new and the old gets smaller, the iteration is said to be *converging*. If delta gets larger, the iteration is said to be *diverging*. The iteration continues until delta reaches a preset amount, or until the

FIGURE 5–4*b* Circular Reference (Formulas for October)

	A	B
5	Circular references used:	Rows 19, 29, and 32
6	Assumptions:	
7	1. Expected monthly interest rate: 0.01	
8	2. Interest income = cash excess * monthly interest rate	
9	3. Interest expense = cash shortage * monthly interest rate	
10		
11	--	
12		Westcoast Import and Export Inc.
13		Cash flow projection
14		For the period 10/1/90 to 12/31/90
15		
16		Oct 90
17	Cash receipts:	
18	Accounts receivable collection	104800
19	Interest income	@IF(B34>0,$B$7*B34,0)
20	Other cash receipts	5000
21		-----------------------
22	Total cash receipts	@SUM(B18:B20)
23		
24	Cash disbursements:	
25	Wages & salaries	60000
26	Rent	10000
27	Selling expenses	17010
28	Advertising	12000
29	Interest expense	@IF(B34<0,-$B$7*B34,0)
30	Other expenses	15000
31		-----------------------
32	Total cash disbursements	@SUM(B25:B30)
33		-----------------------
34	Cash excess (shortage)	+B22-B32
35		=======================

prescribed iteration count has been reached. Most programs allow the user to set the size of delta and the number of iterations.

5.7 GUIDELINES FOR ITERATION

- *Specify the size of delta* for each type of spreadsheet. The delta amount should match the accuracy of the smallest number in spreadsheet. For example, for spreadsheets holding financial figures accurate to the nearest cent, the delta should be set to 0.01.

- *Set number of iterations to infinity (or automatic).* Check to make sure that the spreadsheet program has this option. If the spreadsheet program requires that you set a fixed number of iterations, set the number to as high a value as the program permits. Setting the number of iterations to infinity (or a very high number) will give the spreadsheet program a better chance of solving the circular reference so that the set delta amount is reached. If the spreadsheet program does not permit the setting of the iteration count, you may need to press the recalculation key until the values in the spreadsheet no longer change.

- *Recalculate.* To ensure that the desired solution has been reached, press the recalculate key (<**F9**> for *Lotus 1-2-3*) several times to ensure that the values involved in the circular reference have finally converged and are no longer changing.

5.8 LOCATING UNWANTED CIRCULAR REFERENCES

If a spreadsheet contains an accidental circular reference, there are several means of identifying it, depending on the program in use.

First, check to see if the spreadsheet program has any built-in cell-auditing feature. If so, make sure you and other users know how to use it. Another option is to purchase an add-in program designed for this purpose. For a large company, it is advisable to use a single add-in program (such as *The Spreadsheet Auditor*, from Computer Associates International) so that users can be uniformly trained.

Procedure for Isolating Circular References

Without a built-in circular reference detection facility or an add-in program, it is still possible to isolate cells containing circular references, even though you may have no idea where they are located. The procedure, which can be quite tedious, is as follows.

1. Load a working copy of the spreadsheet containing the unwanted circular reference.

2. Move the cursor to the lowest row containing formulas. Delete this row and see if the circular reference warning indicator is removed. If not, repeat this step until it is. Note the row number, and clear the spreadsheet.

3. Reload an original copy of the spreadsheet and examine the formulas in the row noted in Step 2. Try to trace all the formulas and see if the circular reference can be identified.

4. If the row found in Step 2 contains too many formulas, and the cell or cells containing circular references cannot easily be identified, reload an original copy of the spreadsheet. This time use the process of eliminating one column at a time, starting with the rightmost column. Delete one column at a time, until the circular reference indicator is removed. Note the column number. This column number and the row number noted in Step 2 would pinpoint one cell using a circular reference.

5. Reload the original copy of the spreadsheet, and correct the formula in the cell identified in Steps 1–4.

6. If more than one cell contains a circular reference, repeat the preceding steps until each circular reference is isolated and corrected.

5.9 GUIDELINES FOR CIRCULAR REFERENCES

Circular references are typically used in spreadsheets designed to perform goal-seeking, but should only be used when there are no other means of solving a spreadsheet problem. The cash flow projection model shown in Figure 5–4 is a simple example of a goal-seeking problem.

When using circular references, include documentation indicating which rows or columns (or which specific cells) include circular references. You and other users of the spreadsheet will be glad someone took the time to provide this information. Cells A5 and B5 in Figure 5–4a contain examples of how intentional circular references should be documented in a spreadsheet.

5.10 NAMED RANGES

A named range is a cell or a range of cells to which a spreadsheet developer has assigned a name for ease of reference. One immediate benefit of named ranges is that the names can convey information about the content of the cells.

Example 1.

In a cash budgeting spreadsheet, cell C5 contains the interest rate. Assigning the name INTEREST to cell C5 makes formulas that refer to the interest rate much clearer.

Example 2.

The following Lotus 1-2-3 formulas calculate the total sales tax payable on sales recorded in cells B15 to B89, applying the sales tax rate stored in cell B10.

```
@SUM(B15:B89)*B10
@SUM(SALES)*TAXRATE
```

The style of the second formula makes it easier to read and understand.

Do not overuse named ranges. A spreadsheet that contains more than about 20 named ranges could require an index as to what each name means and where its cells are located. If the named ranges obscure rather than clarify the meaning of formulas, they are not serving their purpose.

Absolute Reference and Named Ranges

If a cell is assigned a name, an absolute cell reference to the cell is also prefaced by a dollar sign ($). For example, if cell B9 is named TAXRATE, then the following forms are equivalent.

```
$B$9
$TAXRATE
```

The <**F4**> key can also be used with named ranges to rotate through the various forms of absolute cell reference. It should be noted that mixed reference cannot be accomplished with named ranges since the named range does not have any means to indicate row and column information.

5.11 GUIDELINES FOR NAMED RANGES

- *Use short names with a specific meaning.*

    Example: Use REVENUE rather than INCOMEINM2.

- *Separate words with underscores.* Check the maximum length of range names permitted by your program. If you need to use a long name or a multiword name, you can separate the words with an underscore.

    Example: Use DEGREESF_TO_C and DEGREESC_TO_F rather than FAHRENTOCENTIGRADE and CENTITOFAHRENHEIT.

- *Do not include blank spaces or the characters* + − * / ^ which could be mistaken for part of a formula.

FIGURE 5–5 Documenting Named Ranges

H	I	J	K	L
11	Named ranges used in this spreadsheet			
12				
13	INTEREST	C5	assumed interest rate	
14	CASH_BAL	C6	required month-end cash balance	
15	REVENUE	B10:M10	12 months projected gross revenue	
16				

- *Avoid function names.* Confusion in formulas could result.

  Example: Do not name a cell (containing an interest rate) INT; in *Lotus 1-2-3*, @INT is the name of a function that returns the integer portion of a number. *SuperCalc5* does not allow you to use the named range INT in a formula.

- *Avoid names that could be read as cell addresses.*

  Example: R2D2, ALL, ME2, BF or CF would all be poor choices. ALL is used by *SuperCalc5* to indicate the entire spreadsheet.

- *Use names only for the key data values.* These are the cells or ranges that are used in many formulas. Be conservative.

  Typically, only a few cells or ranges are referenced in a spreadsheet, and only these need to be named.

- *Document the names and the ranges.* Include in the documentation area a list of the names used in the spreadsheet, their meaning, and the cells to which they correspond. Figure 5–5 shows one way to document named ranges used in a spreadsheet.

Example.

Figure 5–6 shows a cash flow projection spreadsheet prepared for La Jolla Tools Rental, a shop that rents power tools and equipment for home renovations and gardening. The spreadsheet includes the main features covered in this chapter.

- relative cell reference

- absolute cell reference

- circular reference

- named ranges

Figure 5–6a shows the spreadsheet, and Figure 5–6b shows the underlying formulas.

FIGURE 5–6a Comprehensive Example (Spreadsheet)

	A	B	C	D	E
2	Circular references in rows 19, 27, 36, 44, and 47				
3	Assumptions:				
4	1. Minimum cash balance desired:	$15,000	(MINCASH)		
5	2. Interest rate for loan balance:	10.00%	(LNINT)		
6	3. Interest rate for cash balance:	5.00%	(CHINT)		
7	4. Beginning loan balance (Qtr 1):	$1,000	(BAL)		
8	5. Income tax rate:	25.00%			
9					
10			La Jolla Tools Rental		
11			Cash Flow Projections		
12					
13			Quarters		
14					
15		1	2	3	4
16					
17	Cash balance, beginning	$10,000	$15,000	$15,000	$15,000
18	Receipts from customers	125,000	150,000	152,000	125,000
19	Interest income	0	570	725	0
20		--------	--------	--------	--------
21	Total available	135,000	165,000	167,000	140,000
22		--------	--------	--------	--------
23	Less disbursements:				
24	Payroll	100,000	100,000	100,000	100,000
25	Income tax	25,000	25,000	25,000	25,000
26	Rent	8,000	9,000	9,000	9,000
27	Interest expense	(1,545)	(405)	0	(184)
28	Other expenses	3,000	5,000	3,500	3,500
29		--------	--------	--------	--------
30	Total disbursements	134,454	138,595	137,500	137,295
31					
32	Minimum cash balance	15,000	15,000	15,000	15,000
33		--------	--------	--------	--------
34	Total cash needed	149,454	153,595	152,500	152,295
35					
36	Excess (deficiency)	(14,454)	11,405	14,500	(12,295)
37		========	========	========	========
38	Financing:				
39	Borrowing (at begin)	14,454	0	0	12,295
40	Repayment (at end)	0	(11,405)	(14,500)	0
41		--------	--------	--------	--------
42	Total financing effect	14,454	(11,405)	(14,500)	12,295
43		--------	--------	--------	--------
44	Cash balance, end	15,000	15,000	15,000	15,000
45		========	========	========	========
46					
47	Line of credit (at end)	$15,454	$4,049	($10,451)	$1,844

FIGURE 5–6*b*   Comprehensive Example (Formulas)

```
                 A                      B                        C
2   Circular references in rows 19, 27, 36, 44, and 47
3   Assumptions:
4   1. Minimum cash balance desired:              $15,000
5   2. Interest rate for line of credit:          10.00%
6   3. Interest rate for bank balance:             5.00%
7   4. Beginning loan balance (Qtr 1):            $1,000
8   5. Income tax rate:                           25.00%
9
10                                            La Jolla Tools Rental
11                                            Cash Flow Projections
12
13                                                  Quarters
14
15                            1                        2
16
17  Cash balance, beginning   10000                    +B44
18    Receipts from customers 125000                   150000
19    Interest income         @IF(B36>0,$CHINT*B36,0)  @IF(C36>0,$CHINT*C36,0)
20                            ---------------------    -----------------------
21  Total available           +B18+B17                 +C18+C17
22                            ---------------------    -----------------------
23  Less disbursements:
24    Payroll                 100000                   100000
25    Income tax              +B24*$C$8                +C24*$C$8
26    Rent                    8000                     9000
27    Interest expense        @IF(B47>0,-LNINT*B47,0)  @IF(C47>0,-$CHINT*C47,0
28    Other expenses          3000                     5000
29                            ---------------------    -----------------------
30    Total disbursements     @SUM(B24..B28)           @SUM(C24..C28)
31
32    Minimum cash balance    +$MINCASH                +$MINCASH
33                            ---------------------    -----------------------
34  Total cash needed         +B30+B32                 +C30+C32
35
36  Excess (deficiency)       +B21-B34                 +C21-C34
37                            =====================    =======================
38  Financing:
39    Borrowing (at begin)    @IF(B36>0,0,-B36)        @IF(C36>0,0,-C36)
40    Repayment (at end)      @IF(B36>0,-B36,0)        @IF(C36>0,-C36,0)
41                            ---------------------    -----------------------
42  Total financing effect    @SUM(B39..B40)           @SUM(C39..C40)
43                            ---------------------    -----------------------
44  Cash balance, end         +B21+B42-B30             +C21+C42-C30
45                            =====================    =======================
46
47    Line of credit (at end) +BAL+B39+B40             +B47+C39+C40
```

The cash flow projection, prepared for the four quarters of the year, is based on several assumptions specified in rows 4 to 8. Each of the amounts of these assumptions are stored in column C, and each amount is a named range. For instance, the minimum cash balance desired for each quarter is stored in cell C4, and is named MINCASH. Likewise, the interest to be paid to the bank for any outstanding loan balance has the interest rate of 10%, stored in cell C5, and is named LNINT.

If there is a positive cash balance in the line of credit, the bank pays interest at the rate of 5 percent (cell C6, named CHINT). The other assumptions are clearly stated in the spreadsheet. Normally, the income tax rate in C8 would be assigned a name for good style. However, in this spreadsheet, we left the name out so that we could demonstrate the effect of absolute cell reference that does not include the use of a named range.

Examine the formulas displayed in Figure 5–6b. In particular, note the formulas in the following rows:

19 (interest income)
27 (interest expense)
32 (minimum cash balance)

The formulas in these rows reference the amounts in the assumptions in rows 4 to 8. Note the use of absolute cell reference and the named ranges. Compare the use of absolute reference to named ranges in these rows with absolute reference in row 25, which does not include named ranges.

The formulas in rows 19 (interest income) and 27 (interest expense) contain circular cell references. For example, the formula in cell B19 is

@IF(B36>0,$CHINT*B36,0)

The cash excess, or deficiency amounts, in cell B36 is dependent on the total cash inflow and cash outflow. The total cash inflow amount, in turn, is dependent on the interest income amount. Thus, a circular relationship exists between the values in cells B36 and cell C6 (CHINT). A similar situation exists for the formulas in row 27.

CHAPTER SIX

Documenting and Protecting Cell Contents

This chapter sets out alternative styles for documenting the contents of spreadsheet cells. Of particular importance in larger spreadsheets is the need to

- Specify the sources of data.

- Set out the assumptions used in calculations.

- Explain the construction and interrelationship of formulas.

Also included in this chapter are recommendations for protecting cell contents, especially formulas, against accidental deletion or overwriting.

The chapter is divided into the following sections:

6.1 Cell noting methods
6.2 Cell noting programs
6.3 Printing spreadsheet formulas and cell notes
6.4 Guidelines for documenting cell contents
6.5 Protecting cell contents

6.1 CELL NOTING METHODS

The need to document is not unique to spreadsheets. For example, many readers add marginal notes to reports, textbooks, or reference manuals. On occasion publishers even formalize this style, printing marginal annotations or cross-references in books such as law manuals, medical texts, or religious publications.

For many small spreadsheets, the formulas are simple and the logic self-evident; they require no additional documentation. Spreadsheets of some complexity are more likely to require some explanation of the underlying logic and assumptions of the formulas. Without such annotation, the spreadsheet may be very difficult to understand or modify later. Notes on the working of the spreadsheet model can often be as helpful to the originator of the spreadsheet as to other users. Some examples are given below.

Examples.

"The effective interest rate calculated in this formula assumes interest is compounded quarterly."

"The inflation rate (7 percent) used in this formula is based on the 1989 average consumer price index published by Federal Reserve."

"The $40,000 value is the average monthly sales quoted in the January 1990 issue of Consumer Electronics, page 22."

There are several common styles for documenting the content of cells:

- *Write notes on the spreadsheet printout.* A problem with this method is that the hard copy printout is not physically part of the spreadsheet and may be mislaid. As changes are made on the spreadsheet, the developer must remember to update both the information in the electronic file and the written comments on the hard copy. The risk of confusion rises in proportion to the number of changes.

- *Write notes in the cells.* Some spreadsheet programs permit notes to be included in cells along with the value or formula. For instance, *Lotus 1-2-3* Release 3 permits this, requiring the note to be separated from the value or formula by a semicolon (;).

- *Write notes in adjacent cells.* This method is appropriate for small spreadsheets and brief comments. Its weakness is that the notes can clutter up the spreadsheet, as well as put constraints on the space available for values and calculation.

- *Write notes in hidden cells.* A variant on the above method is to place all notes in cells that are adjacent to the cells they document, then hide the columns containing the notes. Hiding the note columns removes the distraction or untidiness of the comments, but raises its own problems: first, hidden columns can interfere with spreadsheet operations such as cursor movements and formula copying; and second, the user must be told about the contents of the hidden columns, resulting in more documentation! The actual operations of hiding and unhiding columns are straightforward and available in most programs.

- *Use a cell noting program.* Unless the spreadsheet program supports cell noting directly, an add-in program may be the best method. Cell notes added in this way are attached to the cells and may be displayed on-screen with the cells, but the notes do not occupy actual cells. The notes are saved and loaded with the spreadsheet, but do not interfere in any way with routine spreadsheet operations.

6.2 CELL NOTING PROGRAMS

A standard cell noting program may be a built-in feature of the spreadsheet program or a separate add-in utility program. It will generally include

- A simple command structure that has a look (*interface*) similar to that of the host spreadsheet.
- A capacity for a large number of notes.
- A basic word processing, editing, and printing capability.
- On-screen indication of which cells have notes attached.
- A list or "map" of notes.
- Automatic move of note along with cell contents when cell location is changed.
- Cut-and-paste between notes and the spreadsheet cells.
- Word search of all cell notes.

More advanced cell noting facilities may include the ability to change the size and position of the cell note window, import text files, link cell references between spreadsheet and related notes, as well as file notes that document the whole spreadsheet, a macro feature, and an unlimited capacity for number or length of notes.

Cautions to observe when considering the use of add-in cell noting programs are as follows.

- Be sure the add-in program is designed for use with your spreadsheet program.

- Check the requirements of the program for disk space and RAM.

- If you want other users to read the comments you have made with the cell noting facility, they must have the same software.

- You should know the method used by the program to store cell notes in your data directory. Although the documentation usually states that the notes are "saved with the spreadsheet," they are probably saved in a separate, linked file. If so, a separate filename will be shown in your data directory, and you must be careful of this when performing any file management cleanup, reorganization, or backup.

Example.

Figure 6–1 shows the use of *Noteworthy*, a *Lotus 1-2-3* add-in from Funk Software, to attach a cell note to a spreadsheet—in this case, cell D6. This cell contains the foreign exchange rate used in the projected income statement for Otus Development Canada Corporation. The cell note, appearing in the pop-up window on the spreadsheet, explains the assumption about the interest rate. The first row of the figure shows the format and content of cell D6 displayed by *Lotus 1-2-3*. The list of six function keys at the top of the screen is part of the *Noteworthy* screen display.

FIGURE 6–1 Example of an On-Screen Cell Note Using Noteworthy

---

```
D6: [W12] 1.21

F1-Help F5-NoteList F6-NoteMap F7-WordLeft F8-WordRight F10-Menu
        A         B          C          D          E          F
6    Exchange rate (Cdn$ to US$):          1.21
7
8    -----------------------------
9                                 ┌─────────────────────────────────
10              Otus Development  │ This exchange rate is determined by
11                     Income s   │ adding 0.05 to the average exchange
12              For the quarter e │ rate for the 12 months ending Dec.
13                                │ 31, 1989.  The exchange rate for
14                                │ second quarter of 1990 is expected
15                                │ to stay around this level.
16   Sales                        │
17   Less: Cost of goods sold     │
18                                │
19   Gross margin                 └═══════════════════════════════D6═
20
```

FIGURE 6–2 Example of a Printed Cell Note

```
D6                          1.21
-------------------------------------------
This exchange rate is determined by
adding 0.05 to the average exchange
rate for the 12 months ending Dec.
31, 1989.  The exchange rate for
second quarter of 1990 is expected to
stay around this level.
-------------------------------------------
```

Figure 6–2 shows an example of a cell note printed by *Noteworthy*. The cell note was entered in Figure 6–1. The printout clearly marks the cell to which the cell note is attached (D6) and the content of the cell (1.21).

6.3 PRINTING SPREADSHEET FORMULAS AND CELL NOTES

Once a spreadsheet has been developed, and after each update, it is good practice to print and file a hard copy. This is particularly important in the following situations.

- If you plan to turn the spreadsheet over to other users for some form of production or presentation, the hard copy serves as a standard and a backup.

- If a spreadsheet file is later suspected of having been corrupted or tampered with, the hard copy is available for verification and correction.

The hard copy of a spreadsheet should include (1) the model, with values shown, (2) the model with cell formulas shown, and (3) the cell notes, if any. For ease of reading and comparison, print cell formulas in the same layout as the spreadsheet; that is, in rows and columns.

Some programs also allow cell formulas to be printed in a two-column list format. This kind of listing is more difficult to use as a reference than the standard row-and-column format. However, it is sometimes useful when formulas are particularly long. (See Chapter 4, Section 4.3, for ways to reduce formula length.)

Figure 6–3 is a two-column listing of cell contents in a *Lotus 1-2-3* spreadsheet (the exchange rate spreadsheet shown in Figure 6–1). Only the formulas in rows 5 to 23 are shown here for purposes of illustration. Note that the second column shows the dis-

---

FIGURE 6–3 Two-Column Listing of Cell Contents (from Figure 6–1)

```
A5:  'Exchange rate (Cdn to US):
D5:  [W12] 1.21
B9:  'Otus Development Canada Corporation
B10: '           Income statement
B11: 'For the quarter ended March 31, 1990
D13: [W12] ^Cdn funds
E13: [W12] ^US funds
A15: 'Sales
D15: (,0) [W12] 2400000
E15: (,0) [W12] +D16/$D$6
A16: 'Less Cost of goods sold
D16: (,0) [W12] 800000
E16: (,0) [W12] +D17/$D$6
D17: [W12] \-
E17: (,0) [W12] \-
A18: 'Gross margin
D18: (,0) [W12] +D16-D17
E18: (,0) [W12] +D19/$D$6
A20: 'Expenses
A21: '   Selling expense
D21: (,0) [W12] 250000
E21: (,0) [W12] +D22/$D$6
A22: '   Office rent
D22: (,0) [W12] 300000
E22: (,0) [W12] +D23/$D$6
A23: '   Salaries
D23: (,0) [W12] 450000
E23: (,0) [W12] +D24/$D$6
```

---

play format and column width, as well as the contents of each cell.

6.4 GUIDELINES FOR DOCUMENTING CELL CONTENTS

The following guidelines will help ensure that cell notes contain the needed information for working with and maintaining the spreadsheet:

- Attach a note to any cell containing values or formulas that need explanation. In case of doubt, it is better to overdocument than to leave users guessing.

- Save cell notes as part of the electronic spreadsheet file and avoid the risks of losing hardcopy documentation. To be doubly sure, print the cell notes also.

- Make cell note information specific to the cell to which it is attached. Locate information that applies to the spreadsheet (such as "global" assumptions) either in the documentation area of the spreadsheet (see Section 4.1) or in an electronic file note.

- For a work group using a common spreadsheet program, adopt a house standard for documenting cell contents. If the spreadsheet program does not have built-in cell noting, provide a standard add-in program for the group.

- When printing the final version of a spreadsheet, also print out (1) the underlying formulas, and (2) all cell notes. Show the cell references for each cell note (see Figure 6–2).

6.5 PROTECTING CELL CONTENTS

Most spreadsheet programs provide some means to prevent accidental erasing or overwriting of cell contents. This is usually achieved by turning on a feature called cell protection, which ensures that the contents of protected cells cannot be changed unless protection is removed. This feature is valuable for cells containing complex formulas. For spreadsheets intended for use by data-entry operators or less experienced users, cell protection is an essential precaution against the risk of operator error.

The following are general guidelines for using cell protection:

- Protect cells that contain data or formulas which are permanent or not subject to frequent change.

- Do not protect cells that are subject to frequent changes, such as cells in data blocks .

- Protect macros, except those that are designed to change their contents during execution.

- Do not protect cells with contents that are changed by macros.

- Take advantage of the different colors available for protected and unprotected blocks if working with a color monitor.

CHAPTER SEVEN

Error-Checking Techniques

To ensure that spreadsheet numbers and computations are accurate, it is good style to build in a systematic means of error checking. This chapter explains guidelines on the design of built-in checks, and provides examples of their application.

The most useful error-checking techniques, and the sections under which they are described are

7.1 Check of row and column totals
7.2 Check of input values with IF and ERR
7.3 Check of missing values with the NA function

Section 7.4 provides guidelines for the use of error-checking techniques.

7.1 CHECK OF ROW AND COLUMN TOTALS

Many financial spreadsheets include a table of values in a row-and-column matrix, with a total at the end of each row and column. The table may also include a grand total that is the sum of all row totals. This grand total should also be the same as the sum of all column totals.

Example.

Figure 7-1a (computed results) and 7-1b (showing part of the formulas) are spreadsheets of the detailed expenses for Milwaukee Discount Electronics during the fourth quarter of 1989,

FIGURE 7–1*a* Comparing Row Totals and Column Totals (Values)

	A	B	C	D	E
1	Demonstrates the comparison of row totals with column totals				
2					
3					
4		Milwaukee Discount Electronics			
5		Detailed Expenses			
6		For the Quarter Oct-89 to Dec-89			
7					
8		Oct 89	Nov 89	Dec 89	Quarter
9					
10	Advertising	$5,000	$6,000	$8,000	$19,000
11	Commissions	12,000	14,000	18,000	44,000
12	Depreciation	1,200	1,200	1,200	3,600
13	Freight	3,000	3,500	4,600	11,100
14	Interests	10,000	10,000	25,000	45,000
15	Rent	65,000	70,000	85,000	220,000
16	Telephone	5,000	5,000	5,000	15,000
17	Wages and benefits	23,000	23,000	23,000	69,000
18		-------------------------------------			
19	Total expenses	124,200	132,700	169,800	426,700
20		=======================================			

including monthly components. Cell B19 is the result of the summing of column B (total expenses for October 1989) and has the formula

@SUM(B10..B17)

Similarly, the formula for cell C19 is

@SUM(C10..C17)

and for cell D19 is

@SUM(D10..D17)

Cells E10 to E17 contain the row totals for rows 10 to 17. For example, cell E10 contains the formula

@SUM(B10..D10)

The formulas in cells E11 to E17 are similar to the one in cell E10.

Cell E19 contains the total expenses for the quarter (grand total). Two possible formulas for cell E19 are

@SUM(B19..D19)
@SUM(E10..E17)

Either of these two formulas will produce the correct grand total, provided that there are no errors in the column totals (cells

---

FIGURE 7–1*b*   Comparing Row Totals and Column Totals (Column E Formulas)

```
        E
        Quarter
8
9
10      @SUM(B10..D10)
11      @SUM(B11..D11)
12      @SUM(B12..D12)
13      @SUM(B13..D13)
14      @SUM(B14..D14)
15      @SUM(B15..D15)
16      @SUM(B16..D16)
17      @SUM(B17..D17)
18      ----------------------------------------------------------
19      @IF(@SUM(B19..D19)=@SUM(E10..E17),@SUM(B19..D19),@ERR)
        ==========================================================
```

B19 to D19) or row totals (cells E10 to E17). However, if there is an error in one of the column or row totals, the grand total in cell E19 may be incorrect, depending upon which formula is used and where the error is.

To eliminate the risk of this error, make use of the IF and ERR functions. For this *Lotus 1-2-3* spreadsheet, the formula in the grand total cell E19 should be (see Figure 7–1*b*)

@IF(@SUM(B19..D19)=@SUM(E10..E17),@SUM(B19..D19),@ERR)

This *error-checking formula* states that if the sum of the column totals is equal to the sum of the row totals, then the former will appear as the grand total. Furthermore, the last part of the formula states that if the two totals are *not* the same, then the grand total cell is to display the indicator ERR. This error check provides the spreadsheet user with the assurance that any grand total that appears has been verified for accuracy. If not, the ERR will indicate the presence of a problem (though not the location of it). For good form, this error checking should be documented in the spreadsheet, preferably in the form of a cell note as described in Chapter 6.

The perceptive reader may have noted that there is still a small risk of error. If there has been an error in the row totals, and this error happens to be the same amount as an error in the column totals, then the grand total could be erroneous. This type of error can only be detected by careful manual verification of computed results.

7.2 CHECK OF INPUT VALUES WITH IF AND ERR

Spreadsheets may be designed so that other users (such as data-entry clerks, sales agents, or students) will input the actual values on which computations are to be based. In such cases, it is good style for the spreadsheet developer to include a means of checking the input values as they are entered.

An error check of this type, for instance, could verify that

- All values are within an acceptable range.
- All values meet some other criterion or criteria.

It is not possible to include an error-checking formula in the cell in which a value is to be entered, as the value would then replace the formula. Two methods can be employed for such checking: placing error checking formulas in an adjoining column, or using a macro to check the data input.

Using the Adjacent Column to Check Input Values

The simplest method for checking for input error is to place error-checking formulas in the adjacent column. If there is a recognizable error in the input data for any cell, the formula will indicate an error condition; otherwise, the adjacent cell will stay blank.

Figure 7–2 illustrates a date-checking technique using an IF function with the ERR function. This technique can be used to check many other kinds of input data. For instance, numeric input values can be checked by a similar style of formula to ensure that the input values fall within an acceptable range.

Example.

Figure 7–2 is an accounts receivable worksheet. Suppose that the accountant feels that it is important to ensure that the invoice dates in column B are entered correctly. A correct invoice date is defined as being less (earlier) than or equal to the current date. Column C contains formulas that check for this error condition. In the example, the current system date (set at bootup time) is November 16, 1989. The formulas in column C check the dates entered by the accounts receivable clerk in column B. If the clerk enters a date greater than the current date, then Column C immediately indicates an error condition. The error-checking formula in cell C7 is:

```
@IF(B7<=@NOW," ",@ERR)
```

FIGURE 7–2   Check of Valid Date Entry

```
          A            B          C              D                    E
1    Accounts receivable worksheet - check for valid date
2
3    Today is:   11/16/1989
4
5    Invoice #     Date                      Customer           Amount
6    --------------------------------------------------------------------
7      890104   11/14/1989      Gracie's Repairs           $145.89
8      890105   11/14/1989      Hemlock Printers           $136.21
9      890106   11/14/1989      Garladi Construction       $274.92
10     890107   11/14/1989      Vander Sam Florist         $341.11
11     890108   11/15/1989      B. Balony & Associates     $184.27
12     890109   11/15/1989      ABC Express Ltd.           $261.63
13     890110   11/15/1989      Jim's Autowreckers         $527.25
14     890111   11/18/1989  ERR SFU & Company Ltd.         $231.64
15     890112   11/16/1989      BC Computers Corp.         $163.74
16     890113   11/16/1989      Pacific Bell               $318.36
17     890114   11/17/1989  ERR Federal Express            $117.42
```

This formula has been copied to the range C8..C17. Cell C7 will display a blank if the date in cell B7 is less than or equal to the current date; otherwise, it will display the ERR indicator. To demonstrate the error check in Figure 7–2, invoice numbers 890111 and 890114 have been given erroneous dates, and the corresponding cells in column C report the error condition.

Example.

Figure 7–3 is a spreadsheet for Antonio's Car Rental, designed to track weekly car rental activities. There are nine cars in the rental fleet. Each Monday morning, the manager enters the beginning and ending odometer reading of any car that has been out in the preceding week. No entry is required for cars not rented, and the odometer entries would be left blank.

To prevent error in data entry, column H of the spreadsheet contains error-checking formulas which verify if the ending odometer reading is less than the beginning reading. For example, cell H13 has the formula:

```
@IF(G13-F13<0,@ERR," ")
```

In Figure 7–3, the entries for the 1989 Chrysler Voyager (row 13) and the 1988 Pontiac Firebird (row 16) contain errors, indicated by the ERR indicator in column H for these two rows. Careful checking of the original rental agreements revealed that the clerk misrecorded the odometer readings on these agreements.

FIGURE 7–3 Error Tracking with the ERR Function

	A	B	C	D	E	F	G	H
1	Antonio's Car Rental							
2								
3	Car rental for the week ended:				15–Oct–89			
4								
5	Car					Odometer	miles	
6	ID	Make and Model		Year	Color	Serial No.	Begin	End
7	--							
8	1	Oldsmobile Cutlass		88	Blue	20941–541	32964	37998
9	2	Ford Mustang		89	Red	F98834–23	17614	19555
10	3	Mercury Cougar		88	Black	M983–942	39523	39903
11	4	Pontiac Firebird		89	Red	P9893–1294	11453	11565
12	5	Buick Skylark		89	Silver	B9834–129	14612	14910
13	6	Chrysler Voyager		89	Maroon	CV978–3494	17813	17791	ERR
14	7	Chrysler Diplomat		89	Black	D9481–32	10314	10545
15	8	Ford Mustang		89	Blue	F86732–43	15151	15666
16	9	Pontiac Firebird		88	Yellow	P9353–1344	30803	30179	ERR

In the case of the Voyager, the ending reading was actually 17,991, whereas for the Firebird, the beginning reading was 20,083.

Checking Input Values with a Macro

If macros are used to control data input into a spreadsheet, it is advisable to include input error-checking in the macro. In fact, there is more flexibility in checking for input errors in macros, since multiple checks can be performed.

Using a macro, it is possible to display the error message in the input cell itself. It is not necessary to display the error condition in another cell as in Figures 7–2 and 7–3. The macro can be used to screen the input value before placing the value into the input cell.

Another alternative is for the macro to display an error message and beep to prompt for correct input, instead of merely indicating the error. This alternative method enables the error check and its correction to be made in the same pass.

Example.

Figure 7–4 is a *Lotus 1-2-3* macro that checks the stock number entered from the keyboard. Only part of the macro is shown here. The macro reads the stock number entered to verify if it is greater than zero and less than 500. If it is not, an error message is dis-

FIGURE 7–4 Checking Input Value with a Macro

```
            /RNCSTOCKNUM~~
            {GETNUMBER "Enter stock number:",STOCKNUM}
AGAIN       {IF STOCKNUM>0#AND#STOCKNUM<500}{BRANCH OK}
            {BEEP}{GETNUMBER "Number out of range -- reenter",STOCKNUM}
            {BRANCH AGAIN}
OK          /RNDSTOCKNUM~
```

played and the operator is prompted, with a beep, to reenter the stock number. A line-by-line explanation follows.

Line 1: Assigns the name STOCKNUM to the current cell.

Line 2: Prompts for input and stores the value in the current cell.

Line 3: Checks the input value. If the value is within the range of 0 to 500, leaves the entered value in the current cell and branches to line 6 (labeled OK) to continue.

Line 4: If the input value is not within the acceptable range, beeps and informs the operator of the error, and prompts for reentry.

Line 5: Branches back to line 3 to check the new input.

Line 6: Removes the name from the current cell after successful completion of the input entry of the stock number.

7.3 CHECK OF MISSING VALUES WITH THE NA FUNCTION

Spreadsheets can be designed as information databases. For example, a spreadsheet can be used as a database for inventory information, for accounts payable, or for accounts receivable. Similar spreadsheet databases can be designed to store information on fixed assets, names and addresses of customers, and so on. (See also Chapter 11 on databases.)

When the information in such spreadsheets is updated, it is possible that some data are missing or not yet available. Often, it would *not* be correct to display a zero in these cells. However, unless you anticipate situations like this in the spreadsheet design, there is a high risk of error, and such error could go undetected for some time.

FIGURE 7–5 Checking for Erroneous Zero Values

	A	B	C	D	E
5					
6			Oficina Inc.		
7			Inventory List		
8					
9		Stock	Unit	Broadway	Store
10	Product	ID	Cost	Quant.	Value
11	---				
12	Dallas chair	CHD 109	57.50	0	.00
13	Bunk bed	BBD 317	350.00	8	2,800.00
14	Cabinet 18x20x34"	CAB 101	126.00	10	1,260.00
15	Cabinet 18x20x54"	CAB 102	187.50	11	2,062.50
16	Conference chair	CHC 208	37.00	0	.00
17	Office desk 48x20"	DKO 121	234.75	9	2,112.75
18	Swivel chair	CHS 215	89.25	12	1,071.00
19	Typewriter table	TBT 110	115.00	16	1,840.00
20	---				
21	Total				11,146.25

Example.

Figure 7–5 is an inventory spreadsheet. In this spreadsheet, the stock counts for Dallas chairs (cell D12) and conference chairs (cell D16) were not yet available when the inventory was last updated. The operator entered zeros in these cells, resulting in an erroneous total inventory value of $11,146.25.

Use of the NA Function

Make it a rule to enter the NA function rather than an erroneous zero when there is missing information for a spreadsheet. The NA (Not Available) display in a cell will alert the reader of the spreadsheet that there is missing information.

Figure 7–6 is a modified version of the inventory spreadsheet in Figure 7–5. Instead of entering zeros in cells D12 and D16, the operator has entered the @NA function. The carrying values in cells E12 and E16 corresponding to these two items automatically change to show NA. Notice that the total inventory value for the Broadway store (cell E21) now also shows NA, meaning that there is missing information in the spreadsheet, and the total value cannot be correctly calculated. Once the @NA functions in cells D12 and D16 are replaced with the actual inventory counts, the formula in cells E12, E16, and E21 will yield correctly calculated values.

FIGURE 7–6 Use of the NA Function

	A	B	C	D	E
5					
6			Oficina Inc.		
7			Inventory List		
8					
9		Stock	Unit	Broadway	Store
10	Product	ID	Cost	Quant.	Value
11	---
12	Dallas chair	CHD 109	57.50	NA	NA
13	Bunk bed	BBD 317	350.00	8	2,800.00
14	Cabinet 18x20x34"	CAB 101	126.00	10	1,260.00
15	Cabinet 18x20x54"	CAB 102	187.50	11	2,062.50
16	Conference chair	CHC 208	37.00	NA	NA
17	Office desk 48x20"	DKO 121	234.75	9	2,112.75
18	Swivel chair	CHS 215	89.25	12	1,071.00
19	Typewriter table	TBT 110	115.00	16	1,840.00
20	---
21	Total				NA

7.4 GUIDELINES FOR ERROR-CHECKING TECHNIQUES

Row and column totals. Whenever row totals and column totals are calculated in a spreadsheet, and a grand total needs to be calculated, always use the IF function to check that the row totals match the column totals.

Checking input values. Built-in input value checking should be used

- When designing spreadsheets for use by other people where the user enters data values into the spreadsheets.

- When designing spreadsheets (for use by the developer or other people) where erroneous data entry can lead to costly mistakes.

Missing values. Spreadsheet cells containing missing values should be set up to display the NA indicator rather than zeros.

CHAPTER EIGHT

Decision-Making Style: Using IF, CHOOSE, and Table Lookup

In constructing some spreadsheet formulas, it is necessary to direct the program to select an appropriate value from several choices. The formula, in effect, makes a decision based on the rules you have built into it. For example, in an income tax planning spreadsheet, after computing the taxable income amount, it is necessary to determine the amount of income tax payable. This may be a simple matter of selecting a tax rate from several alternatives, or it may require the program to look up the tax payable directly from a given table of values.

The correct style for making choices of this nature is to use one or more of the following functions described in this chapter:

The IF function (Sections 8.1 to 8.4)
The CHOOSE function (Section 8.5)
The table lookup functions (Section 8.6)

Sometimes these functions are interchangeable; at other times, one may be more appropriate than the others. Section 8.7 provides guidelines.

8.1 THE IF FUNCTION

The IF function is designed to make a decision between two choices. In a simple form, it can test whether the value in any given cell belongs to one of two categories, then take a specified action determined by the outcome of the test. The IF function requires three arguments to be specified, in the form:

IF (logical expression, action if true, action if false)

As will be demonstrated in Section 8.2, the IF function can be made more complex by nesting one function within another, by means of more sets of parentheses. But first, we present an example of a straightforward IF function.

Example.

Figure 8–1a (displaying results) and Figure 8–1b (displaying formulas) illustrate the use of an IF formula to assign a product in an inventory list to one of two categories. In this store there are two categories of product, each with a different markup factor. Thus

For Category 1, the markup factor is 1.5.
For Category 2, the markup factor is 2.5.

The formulas in column E determine the markup factor. For example, cell E12 contains the formula (see Figure 8–1b)

@IF(C12=1,1.5,2.5)

Since cell C12 contains a value of 1 (that is, Dallas chair is of category 1), the markup factor yielded by the IF function is 1.5.

FIGURE 8–1a Choosing from Two Alternatives (Values)

	A	B	C	D	E	F
			Oficina Inc.			
			Inventory List			
6						
7						
8						
9		Stock	Product	Unit	Markup	Retail
10	Product	ID	Category	Cost	Factor	Price
11	--					
12	Dallas chair	CHD 109	1	57.50	1.5	86.25
13	Bunk bed	BBD 317	2	350.00	2.5	875.00
14	Cabinet 18x20x34"	CAB 101	1	126.00	1.5	189.00
15	Cabinet 18x20x54"	CAB 102	1	187.50	1.5	281.25
16	Conference chair	CHC 208	1	37.00	1.5	55.50
17	Office desk 48x20"	DKO 121	2	234.75	2.5	586.88
18	Swivel chair	CHS 215	2	89.25	2.5	223.13
19	Typewriter table	TBT 110	1	115.00	1.5	172.50

FIGURE 8–1b   Choosing from Two Alternatives (Column E Formulas)

	A	B	C	D	E
			Oficina Inc.		
6					
7			Inventory List		
8					
9		Stock	Product	Unit	Markup
10	Product	ID	Category	Cost	Factor
11	---				
12	Dallas chair	CHD 109	1	57.50	@IF(C12=1,1.5,2.5)
13	Bunk bed	BBD 317	2	350.00	@IF(C13=1,1.5,2.5)
14	Cabinet 41x68	CAB 101	1	126.00	@IF(C14=1,1.5,2.5)
15	Cabinet 80x126	CAB 102	1	187.50	@IF(C15=1,1.5,2.5)
16	Conference chair	CHC 208	1	37.00	@IF(C16=1,1.5,2.5)
17	Office desk 160x75	DKO 121	2	234.75	@IF(C17=1,1.5,2.5)
18	Swivel chair	CHS 215	2	89.25	@IF(C18=1,1.5,2.5)
19	Typewriter table	TBT 110	1	115.00	@IF(C19=1,1.5,2.5)
20	---				

8.2 NESTED IF FUNCTION

The IF function can be nested. That is, multiple conditions can be set up by placing a second IF function inside another IF function. It is possible for several layers of IF functions to be layered, one within the other. This style of IF function enables you to set up a spreadsheet to make the kind of choices demonstrated in the following example.

Example.

The inventory spreadsheets in Figures 8–1a and 8–1b could be modified to have three categories of products for the purposes of applying different markups. You would want the formulas in column E to decide the markup factor for each category according to the following logic:

STEP 1 If the product category is 1, yield the markup factor of 1.5.

STEP 2 If the product category is 2, yield the markup factor of 2.5.

STEP 3 If the product category is 3, yield the markup factor of 3.5.

The formula in cell E12 would then read:

```
@IF(C12=1,1.5,@IF(C12=2,2.5,3.5))
```

8.3   ERROR CHECK FOR IF FUNCTIONS

It is a relatively simple matter to build an error check into formulas using an IF function. (See also Chapter 7 on general error-checking techniques.)

Example.

This example is based on the retail markup spreadsheet used in Figure 8–1*b*. The following IF formula commits a common error of omission:

```
@IF(C12=1,1.5,@IF(C12=2,2.5,3.5))
```

Note that the logic of this formula actually proceeds as follows:

> If cell C12 has a value of 1, display the markup of 1.5; otherwise, if the value in C12 is 2, display the markup of 2.5; otherwise, display the markup of 3.5.

The flaw in the formula is that, for any value other than 1 or 2 entered as the product category in cell C12, the formula yields the default value of 3.5. Clearly, this would be inaccurate. Thus, if a value greater than 3 were entered by error in C12, there would be no indication of that error in the spreadsheet. A proper use of the IF function, in this case, should be:

```
@IF(C12=1,1.5,@IF(C12=2,2.5,@IF(C12=3,3.5,@ERR)))
```

Note the care that must be taken with parentheses in nested functions of any kind. The rule of thumb is to count that there are as many opening (right-facing) parentheses as there are closing (left-facing) parentheses. This formula explicitly checks for each of the product categories. Any value other than the given categories will result in an error value appearing in the cell.

8.4   INPUT BLOCK FOR IF FUNCTIONS

In the previous two examples (Sections 8.2 and 8.3), in order to focus on the decision-making techniques, we used the simplest form of the IF function by embedding the markup values right in the formulas. However, a better style is to place the markup factors in an input block and reference these values by cell address.

Example.

For example, Figure 8–2 is an improved style of spreadsheet where the markup factors of 1.5, 2.5, and 3.5 are entered into an input block A3..B5. Thus, the formulas in column E refer to these values

FIGURE 8–2 Input Block for an IF Function

	A	B	C	D	E	F
3	Category 1 markup:		1.5			
4	Category 2 markup:		2.5			
5	Category 3 markup:		3.5			
6			Oficina Inc.			
7			Inventory List			
8						
9		Stock	Product	Unit	Markup	Retail
10	Product	ID	Category	Cost	Factor	Price
11	--					
12	Dallas chair	CHD 109	1	57.50	1.5	86.25
13	Bunk bed	BBD 317	2	350.00	2.5	875.00
14	Cabinet 18x20x34"	CAB 101	1	126.00	1.5	189.00
15	Cabinet 18x20x54"	CAB 102	1	187.50	1.5	281.25
16	Conference chair	CHC 208	1	37.00	1.5	55.50
17	Office desk 48x20"	DKO 121	2	234.75	2.5	586.88
18	Swivel chair	CHS 215	2	89.25	2.5	223.13
19	Typewriter table	TBT 110	1	115.00	1.5	172.50

rather than having them embedded. For instance, the formula in E13 is:

`@IF(C12=1,B3,@IF(C12=2,B4,@IF(C12=3,B5,@ERR)))`

A further improvement is to use absolute cell reference (see Section 5.3) so that this formula can be copied to other cells in column E without any modifications:

`@IF(C12=1,$B$3,@IF(C12=2,$B$4,@IF(C12=3,$B$5,@ERR)))`

The benefit to the spreadsheet user appears when the retailer decides to change the markup factors. The new markup factors only need to be entered in cells B3 to B5; no formula modifications are required.

8.5 THE CHOOSE FUNCTION

The CHOOSE function provides for a different, and often simpler, style of decision-making formula: it requires a choice to be made from a number of alternatives. In cases of more than two alternatives, it is much easier to set up than the corresponding formula using the IF function.

The general form of the CHOOSE function is:

`CHOOSE(key,choice₀,choice₁,choice₂, choice₃,...,choiceₙ)`

The CHOOSE function uses the key as a criterion for making the decision between the choices listed in the formula. The key must be a whole number or a cell reference that contains a whole number. The number of choices must correspond to the maximum value of the key. The choices must be listed consecutively. Note that the first choice is listed as $choice_0$ not $choice_1$. Another point to remember about the CHOOSE function is that if the key does not match any of the choices, the error indicator ERR will be displayed in the cell.

Example.

In the spreadsheet shown in Figure 8–1a, the following formula could be placed in cell E12 instead of the IF function:

@CHOOSE(C12–1,1.5,2.5,3.5)

meaning:

> Look at the key value in cell C12 and subtract 1 from it. Then use that value to find a match from the choices provided; that is, $choice_0$ = 1.5, $choice_1$ = 2.5, and $choice_2$ = 3.5).

The value of 1 is subtracted from C12 because the @CHOOSE function starts the choices at an index value of 0. Should the value in C12 not match any of the three choices, the CHOOSE function displays the error condition ERR in cell E12.

The CHOOSE function can be used where the key value does not have consecutive values. For example, if the product categories are 1, 2, 4, and 6, yielding the markups of 1.5, 2.5, 3.5, and 4.5, respectively, then the following formula can be used:

@CHOOSE(C12–1,1.5,2.5,@ERR,3.5,@ERR,4.5)

The choices corresponding to the nonexisting product categories of 3 and 5 yield the error indicator ERR. Alternatively, the @NA function can be used, thus:

@CHOOSE(C12–1,1.5,2.5,@NA,3.5,@NA,4.5)

This displays the NA indicator if there is no category.

If there are a large number of choices, or the choices are in no particular order, the CHOOSE function can become quite complicated and is therefore not recommended. For such cases, consider using a table lookup function (see Section 8.6).

FIGURE 8–3 Table Lookup

	A	B	C	D	E	F	G	H
6				Oficina Inc.				
7				Inventory List				
8								
9		Product	Unit	Markup	Retail		Markup table	
10	Product	Category	Cost	Factor	Price			
11	--						Cat.	Markup
12	Dallas chair		1	57.50	1.25	71.88	1	1.25
13	Bunk bed		3	350.00	2.00	700.00	2	1.50
14	Cabinet 18x20x34"		1	126.00	1.25	157.50	3	2.00
15	Cabinet 18x20x54"		4	187.50	2.50	468.75	4	2.50
16	Conference chair		2	37.00	1.50	55.50	5	3.50
17	Office desk 48x20		1	234.75	1.25	293.44		
18	Swivel chair		4	89.25	2.50	223.13		
19	Typewriter table		5	115.00	3.50	402.50		

8.6 TABLE LOOKUP FUNCTIONS

A table lookup function provides a way of getting the program to look up values from a supplied table of values laid out in adjacent columns or rows of the spreadsheet. Most spreadsheet programs provide at least two table lookup functions: one for looking up a "vertical" table set up in columns, the other for looking up a horizontal table set up in rows. *Lotus 1-2-3*, for instance, the corresponding functions are @VLOOKUP and @HLOOKUP.

The general forms of these functions are:

```
@VLOOKUP(value,range,column offset)
@HLOOKUP(value,range,row offset)
```

In the case of @VLOOKUP, the function looks up the value in the leftmost column of the range specified; it then moves over the number of columns specified as the "offset," and returns that value to the cell. The procedure is similar for @HLOOKUP, except that rows are used for the lookup.

Example.

Figure 8–3 is an inventory spreadsheet that uses the @VLOOKUP function to determine the appropriate markup for a product. Cell D12, for example, has the formula:

```
@VLOOKUP(B12,$G$12..$H$16,1)
```

meaning:

FIGURE 8–4 Table Lookup (Ranges of Values)

	A	B	C	D	E	F	G
6			Oficina Inc.				
7			Inventory List				
8							
9		Unit	Markup	Retail		Markup table:	
10	Product	Cost	Factor	Price		Price	
11	--					range	Markup
12	Dallas chair	57.50	1.30	74.75		$10	1.25
13	Bunk bed	350.00	3.00	1,050.00		$50	1.30
14	Cabinet 18x20x34"	126.00	2.10	264.60		$70	1.70
15	Cabinet 18x20x54"	187.50	2.50	468.75		$120	2.10
16	Conference chair	37.00	1.25	46.25		$150	2.50
17	Office desk 48x20"	234.75	2.80	657.30		$200	2.80
18	Swivel chair	89.25	1.70	151.73		$300	3.00
19	Typewriter table	115.00	1.70	195.50			

Look up the value in B12 in the markup table G12..H16, and return the markup from one column to the right (column H) in the table.

Table Lookup For Ranges of Values

Actually, the lookup functions do not perform a one-to-one match, as do the IF and CHOOSE functions. In the case of vertical lookup, the value to be looked up is compared to the leftmost column of the table, which must be sorted in ascending order.

Example.

Figure 8–4 demonstrates this feature of the lookup function. The formula in cell C12 reads:

```
@VLOOKUP(B12,$F$12..$G$18,1)
```

That is, the value in cell B12 is looked up in the markup table F12..G18. The markup depends on the unit cost of the product. If the product cost equals or is less than $10, the markup factor is 1.25. If the product costs between 10 and 50 dollars, the markup factor is 1.30, and so on. Notice that in this example, the lookup is performed over a range of values, rather than being a lookup of specific values.

Table Lookup For Specific Values

Some applications require that a specific value be looked up in a table or database. If an exact match is found in the table, then a

FIGURE 8–5 Specific Value Lookup

```
        A          B              C                  D
5    Table lookup of a repair item
6    Repair claim ticket number:           1653
7    Serial number:                        361349
8    Name of equipment:                    Zenith Z-248 PC
9    Repair depot:                         West Palm Beach
10   -------------------------------------------------------------
11                        Florida Revivals Inc.
12                        Equipment Repair List
13   Claim
14   Ticket   Serial
15   Number   Number         Equipment        Repair depot
16   -------------------------------------------------------------
17   1356     B425679     IBM Selectric        Boca Raton
18   1367     21PS32156   IBM PS/2 Model 50    Ft. Lauderdale
19   1468     7714185Y    Sony Video Monitor   Boca Raton
20   1653     361349      Zenith Z-248 PC      West Palm Beach
21   1876     87DP51241   Compaq Deskpro       Biscayne Bay
22   2163     412364      Olivetti Electric    Ft. Lauderdale
```

corresponding value is returned from the table. But if there is no exact match, the lookup process should return an error message.

Example.

Figure 8–5 is an equipment repair list for Florida Revivals Inc., which has several office equipment repair depots in Florida. Depending on the availability of repair specialists, equipment sent in by customers may be shipped to a particular repair depot for repair work. The spreadsheet is designed so that the location and name of any particular piece of equipment can be identified quickly to answer customer queries, given the claim ticket number provided by the customer.

For illustrative purposes, only part of the repair list is shown in Figure 8–5. The formulas in cells D7 to D9 look up the particulars for the equipment with the claim ticket number given in cell D6.

To perform an exact lookup, the formulas are:

```
D7:  @IF(D6=@VLOOKUP(D6,A16..D21,0),
         @VLOOKUP(D6,A16..D21,1),@ERR)
D8:  @IF(D6=@VLOOKUP(D6,A16..D21,0),
         @VLOOKUP(D6,A16..D21,2),@ERR)
D9:  @IF(D6=@VLOOKUP(D6,A16..D21,0),
         @VLOOKUP(D6,A16..D21,3),@ERR)
```

In each of these formulas, the serial number in cell D6 is first exactly matched to an entry in the table by comparing the serial number with the leftmost column in the table. For example, the first step for the formula in cell D7 is:

`D6=@VLOOKUP(D6,A16..D21,0)`

If there is an exact match, the IF function performs the table lookup in the appropriate column, thus:

`@VLOOKUP(D6,A16..D21,1)`

If there is no exact match, the IF function yields the ERR value.

In Figure 8–5, if the claim ticket number in cell D6 does not match any of the claim ticket numbers in the repair list, cells D7, D8, and D9 will all display the error value ERR. Note that without the use of the IF function, the VLOOKUP will return values to cells D7, D8, and D9, even if there is no such claim ticket number in the list.

8.7 GUIDELINES FOR USING IF, CHOOSE, AND TABLE LOOKUP FUNCTIONS

- Use the IF function only when a small number of choices (two or three) are present. When there are a large number of choices, consider using the CHOOSE function or a table lookup function.

- When using the IF function, the formula must explicitly check all conditions. The formula should display an error value if none of the conditions are met.

- Use the CHOOSE function if the choices are in consecutive order, and when there are more than two or three (but not more than five or six) choices.

- Avoid the CHOOSE function when the choices are in no particular order, or where there are a large number of gaps between the choices. For such cases, consider using a table lookup.

- Use table lookup functions when there is a large number of choices, or when ranges of values rather than specific values are to be looked up.

- Where an exact match is required, use the IF function in conjunction with the lookup function.

CHAPTER NINE

Macros, Menus, and User-Defined Functions

Most spreadsheet programs provide a feature called a macro that performs a repetitive sequence of tasks in response to a single user command. The three most common types of macros are:

- To record and replay a sequence of keystrokes.

- To control spreadsheet operations.

- To build custom applications such as menus or dialog boxes.

This chapter describes an effective style for using macros, and provides guidelines for the use of custom menus (including dialog boxes) and user-defined functions. The sections are organized as follows:

NOTE: All macro examples in this chapter are based on the macro features provided in *Lotus 1-2-3*, Releases 2.01 and 2.2. The dialog box examples are derived from *Microsoft Excel*.

FIGURE 9–1   Printing Macro with Three-Column Layout

	A	B	C
13	\P	/PPCA	Clear all previous print settings
14		RA1.G45~	Set the print range
15		OF1990 Budget~Q	Specify footer on each page
16		G	Start printer

9.1   TYPES OF MACROS

Macros to Record and Replay Keystrokes

The macro effectively stores a sequence of keystrokes that can be replayed later by entering a single command. Keystrokes may include cursor movements and spreadsheet commands.

Example.

Figure 9–1 is a macro that prints a spreadsheet with a footer on every page. Similar macros can print spreadsheets in different formats, or format cells in a particular style.

Macros to Control Spreadsheet Operations

The macro stores commands that control the operation of the spreadsheet. It may also prompt for input from the keyboard, and automatically follow branching instructions in response to that input. This type of macro can accurately perform quite complicated procedures that might otherwise run the risk of error, and is therefore suitable for end users who may know only a few basic commands.

Example.

Figure 9–2 is an example of this type of a macro that sorts a database in three different ways.

Macros to Build Custom Applications

Macros can be used to customize applications so that users of spreadsheets developed by others do not need to know any spreadsheet commands at all. Advanced macros can present the operator with custom menus or dialog boxes.

Example.

Figure 9–4 is a macro with a custom menu. By selecting choices from the menu, the user can perform data management operations on an inventory list.

FIGURE 9–2 Sorting Macro (Comments Column Not Shown)

```
         A                      B
60  \KEY
61  \M              /DSRDDATABASE~Q
62                  {GETLABEL "Sort by Product (P), Stock count (S), or Cost (C) ",\KEY}
63                  {IF \KEY="P"}{BRANCH \SORTP}
64                  {IF \KEY="S"}{BRANCH \SORTS}
65                  {IF \KEY="C"}{BRANCH \SORTC}
66
67  \SORTP          /DSPA1~A~G
68                  {BRANCH \CLEAN}
69
70  \SORTS          /DSPB1~A~G
71                  {BRANCH \CLEAN}
72
73  \SORTC          /DSPC1~A~G
74  \CLEAN          /RE\KEY~
```

Explanation:

Line 60	Contains the named range \KEY used to store the keyboard input.
Line 61	First command of the \M macro, resets the sorting parameters and sets the sort range to the named range DATABASE.
Line 62	Prompts the user to enter P, S, or C to specify sort sequence.
Line 63 to 65	Checks the user response and branch to the appropriate labels.
Line 67	Sorts by column A which contains product names.
Line 68	Branches to clean up before exit from macro.
Line 70	Sorts by column B which contains stock counts.
Line 71	Branches to clean up before exit from macro.
Line 73	Sorts by column C which contains product costs.
Line 74	Cleans up before exit from macro.

9.2 GUIDELINES FOR MACRO STYLE

The following ten guidelines for macro style have been found to improve the reliability of all types of spreadsheet macros.

Macro layout. Use a three-column layout for all macros. In the left column, enter the labels for the macro and the macro instructions. In the center column, enter the sequence of instructions. In the right column, enter comments documenting the logic and flow of the macro instructions. Figure 9–1 is a printing macro with the recommended three-column layout.

Macro names. Always assign names to macros so that they can be located easily by a spreadsheet developer or user. If macros are assigned names, they can be located by listing the named ranges on-screen (often by just pressing a function key). Some spreadsheet programs do not require a macro to be named; unnamed macros are executed by specifying the start cell address. However, it is still good style to name them, for the reasons previously stated.

Spreadsheet programs have rules for the style of macro names. Some (e.g., *Lotus 1-2-3* Releases 2.2 and 3) allow several characters to be used; others restrict macro names to single characters; (e.g., *Lotus 1-2-3*, Release 2.01). In the latter case, it is good style to precede the macro name with a backslash (\) so that macros can easily be distinguished in the list of named ranges in the spreadsheet.

Never give a macro the same name as a built-in function. For instance, it would be poor style to name a macro FV, which could easily be confused with the future value function FV.

Label names. When a macro contains branching instructions, it is necessary to attach a label to each branch so that the program can identify it as such. It is good style to precede labels with a backslash (\) to make them easier to identify. Since most spreadsheet programs permit multicharacter labels, select meaningful names for these labels.

Figure 9–2 is a sorting macro with multiple labels. The comments column has been omitted. The main macro is named \M, and the branches are named \SORTP (sort by product), \SORTS (sort by stock count), \SORTC (sort by cost), and \CLEAN (clean up before exiting). A brief explanation of the macro is included in the lower half of this macro block.

Document the macro. Figure 9–1 demonstrates the importance of documentation. Use a comment column to explain how each command in the macro works. Without documentation, even simple macros are very hard to understand and modify. For complicated macros, use cell noting for individual macro cells, and add a comments column. To keep documentation simple, limit the number of operations entered in each cell of the macro. (See also Chapter 6 on documenting cell contents.)

Keep commands short and simple. The correct style is to keep a command to no more than two or three operations. A long command is hard to understand and even harder to debug if it has an error.

Most spreadsheet programs permit a macro command entered in a cell to be as many characters as the cell can hold, which can be as many as several hundred characters. It is poor style to enter a command that is longer than a screen width, since this makes it difficult to read and understand. Documentation also becomes unwieldy.

In Figure 9–1, the print command is split into four steps, each step being contained in one cell of the macro.

In Figure 9–2, each command in the macro performs no more than three functions, rendering the macro commands easy to understand and modify.

Override default settings. Commands used in macros should not assume any default settings, or rely on the settings of a previous operation. It is good style to reset all default settings, and then specify each parameter in the macro. The macro in Figure 9–1 starts by resetting the printing defaults. Similarly, the macro in Figure 9–2 starts the sort operation by resetting all parameters.

There are two reasons for this style. First, the behavior of the macro will not depend on the results of a previous operation, which could be inappropriate for the current one. Second, the macro is easy to understand and modify since there are no hidden conditions or settings on which the macro relies.

Clean up before exit. Before exiting from a macro, it is good style to erase any temporary information used during macro execution. By cleaning up before exit, the macro will leave no transient information in the spreadsheet that might confuse another user. This is particularly important with complex macros that may include many temporary variables or named ranges.

In Figure 9–2, the cleanup step is included even though the macro is relatively simple. The last line of the macro removes the temporary keyboard value from cell B60 (\KEY) before exiting from the macro. If this is not done, cell B60 would contain the keyboard entry left behind after the last use of the macro and might puzzle the next user.

Keep macros simple. In designing macros for easy understanding and maintenance, it is essential to keep the macro simple. Always prefer a direct route to a circuitous one. For example, in designing an input macro, after displaying the on-screen prompt for keyboard input, have the macro place the cursor in the cell where the data are to be entered. This is better style than having the data input to the cell next to the question, and then having the response copied to the target cell.

Built-in error checking. Where possible, build in error checks to assure the accuracy of information entered from the keyboard. You can use one of the methods described in Chapter 7, or build in an error check as part of the macro.

FIGURE 9–3 Checking for Input Error

	F	G	H
45	\I	{GETNUMBER "Enter age of retirement: ",\AGE}	
46		{IF \AGE<55#OR#\AGE>72}{BRANCH \WRONGAGE}	
47			
60	\WRONGAGE	{GETNUMBER "Age is out of range -- reenter: ",\AGE}	

Figure 9–3 is part of a macro that is designed to check for input error. Error checking is performed in cell G46. In the related spreadsheet, retirement age must be greater or equal to 55, and less than 72 in order to quality for the special retirement benefit. If the age entered is out of the valid range, the user is asked (in cell G60) to enter the correct information. (See also Chapter 7 on error checking.)

Save before testing. After a macro is created, and before it is put to the test, make it a rule to save the spreadsheet first. Unless the macro is perfect, there is a risk that the macro may change or damage the spreadsheet in some unexpected manner.

9.3 CUSTOM MENUS

By providing them with custom on-screen *menus*, developers can present untrained operators with spreadsheets that perform complicated operations that they can operate without risk. The creation of this type of macro is called *macro programming*. It is an advanced set of spreadsheet skills and techniques beyond the scope of this book. However, an example will indicate the effectiveness of this style of macro.

Example.
Figure 9–4 is a macro that presents a custom menu to the user. The macro displays four menu choices on-screen, in the dialog area of the spreadsheet:

```
Add   Sort   Print   Quit
```

Associated with each menu choice is a help message, displayed in the second line as the cursor highlights the choice. The user only has to move the cursor to the desired choice and press ‹**Enter**› or press the first letter of the desired choice. The macro controls

FIGURE 9–4   Custom Menu with Macro

	H	I	J	K	L
1	\0	{MENUBRANCH \TOP}			
2		{BRANCH \A}			
3					
4	\TOP	Add	Sort	Print	Quit
5		Add more records	Sort records	Print inventory	Save and exit
6		{BRANCH \ADD}	{BRANCH \ST}	{BRANCH \PP}	{BRANCH \SE}
7					
8	\ADD	{GOTO}DATABASE~		Move cursor to top of data block	
9		{END}{DOWN}{DOWN}		Move to blank row at bottom of data block	
10		{?}~{RIGHT}		Wait for input of product name	
11		{?}~{RIGHT}		Wait for input of stock ID	
12		{?}~{RIGHT}		Wait for input of unit cost	
13		{?}~{RIGHT}		Wait for input of quantity in Store #1	
14		{UP}/C~{DOWN}~{DOWN}{RIGHT}		Copy formula to calculate carrying value	
15		{?}~{RIGHT}		Wait for input of quantity in Store #2	
16		{UP}/C~{DOWN}~{DOWN}		Copy formula to calculate carrying value	
17		/RNCDATABASE~{DOWN}~		Extend data area to include new record	
18		{BRANCH \A}			
19					
20	\ST	/DSRDDATABASE~		Clear and set sort range to data area	
21		PA1~A~G		Sort by column A (product name)	
22		{BRANCH \A}			
23					
24	\PP	/PPCR		Clear print range	
25		RDATABASE~GQ		Set print range to data area and print	
26		{BRANCH \A}			
27					
28	\SE	/FS~R		Save file and replace old copy	
29		/QY		Exit to DOS	

the operation of the spreadsheet, including adding new inventory records, sorting the data, printing the updated inventory list, and saving the spreadsheet before exiting to DOS.

The macro (named \ 0) is an autoexec macro. That is, the macro executes automatically when the spreadsheet is loaded by the user. Column K displays detailed documentation for each of the menu choices.

9.4   GUIDELINES FOR MENUS

Names of menu choices.   Each choice on the menu should have a unique first letter so that the user can select a choice by pressing one letter rather than moving the cursor. Use a single word for each choice if possible, and explain the choice in the help message associated with the choice. In any case, use as few words as possible for a menu choice so as not to clutter the screen.

Help message. The help message should not repeat the menu choice. Instead, it should explain the action that the menu choice performs.

Number of menu choices. Keep the number of menu choices small. No more than seven choices should be presented in one menu. If more than seven choices are needed, organize the choices so that several choices can be displayed in a second-level menu.

For example, in Figure 9–4, if several ways of sorting are desired, then display a *submenu* when the user selects the "Sort" choice in the master menu. In the submenu, set out the various means of sorting. Most spreadsheet programs permit the use of multiple levels of menus. If more than one level of menu choice is used, always include a choice in the submenu to return the user to the higher level menu.

Structure. Most spreadsheet programs allow macro commands to be placed in the cells in the same column right after the help message of a menu choice. As a matter of good style, always place macro commands in a separate block of the spreadsheet, and use the BRANCH command to direct the macro to execute the commands. For example, in Figure 9–4, the sort instructions start in cell J6 with a BRANCH command.

Each menu choice has a branch command in row 6 that directs the macro to the appropriate portion of the macro to execute the selected choice. Use of this style has three advantages. First, it enables the macro commands to have a comments column, which is not the case if the macro commands immediately follow the macro choice. Second, the macro commands are easier to read, since they would overlap each other if they were in adjacent columns. Third, changes can more readily be made to the macro commands.

9.5 CUSTOM DIALOG BOXES

Some spreadsheet programs permit the design of custom dialog boxes. Dialog boxes are used along with macros, allowing on-screen interaction with the user. Using a dialog box, each input field can be given a name or a prompt. The user enters the information in the space provided in the dialog box.

Figure 9–5 is a dialog box designed with *Microsoft Excel*. The dialog box facilitates entry of a new item into the inventory of a store.

Figure 9–5 Custom Dialog Box

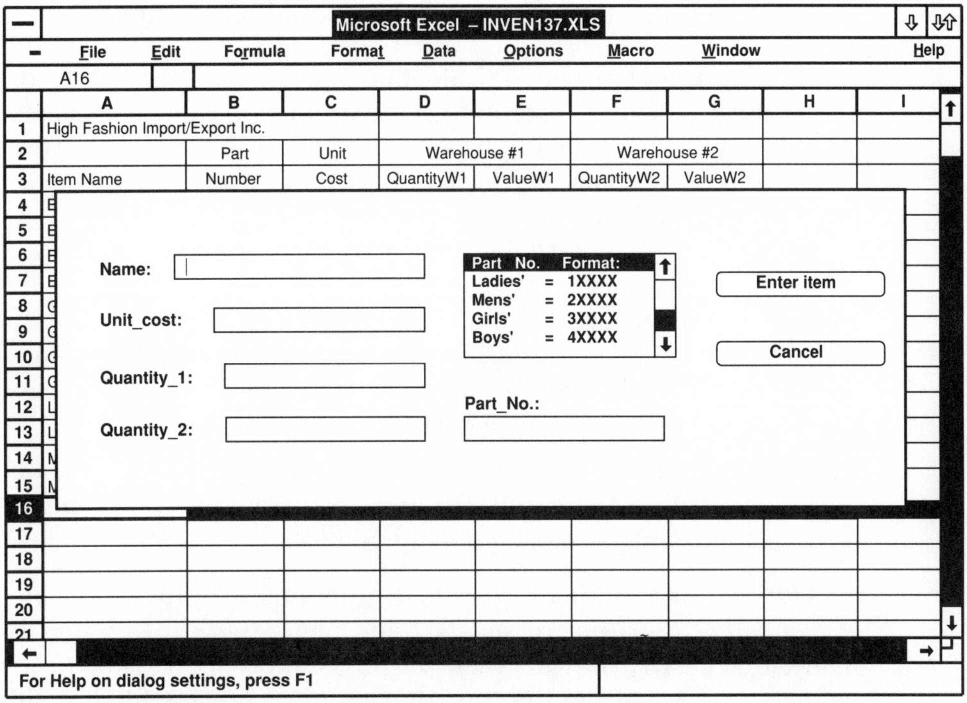

9.6 GUIDELINES FOR DIALOG BOXES

Keep the dialog box simple. Include no more than six or seven items in a dialog box. If more than six or seven items need to be entered, use more than one dialog box.

Use meaningful labels. Label each input box with a meaningful label. In Figure 9–5, the dialog box has five items, each labeled clearly.

Provide on-screen help. If possible, include lists or reminder messages in the dialog box to facilitate data input. In Figure 9–5, the Part No. Format box is used to list the format of part numbers, reminding the operator of the first digit of the four inventory categories.

9.7 USER-DEFINED FUNCTIONS

Some spreadsheet programs permit functions to be created and added to the program. *Microsoft Excel*, for example, permits users to add their own functions to perform calculations that cannot easily be performed by the built-in functions. In designing user defined functions, the following rules should be considered.

Naming convention. Within the constraints imposed by the spreadsheet program, user-defined functions should have names that clearly indicate their purpose and follow a standard format. For example, the name SALES.COMMISSION may be given to a function that performs this calculation.

Ownership may also be indicated. For example, the functions might have names that start with the initials of the responsible spreadsheet developer or the department. This is particularly important for work groups. For example, the function name ACC.SALES.COMMISSION indicates that the sales commission spreadsheet belongs to the accounting group.

Documentation. User-defined functions, like macros, must be documented. Use the combination of cell notes and a comment column to provide adequate documentation.

Library. Keep all user-defined functions in a library of files (*Excel* calls these "macro sheets") and name these files with filenames that clearly indicate their purposes. If possible, collect user-defined macros of similar functions into a special file for this purpose.

CHAPTER TEN

Multiple, Linked, and 3-D Spreadsheets

This chapter provides guidelines for the design of a group of spreadsheets with interrelated data that the user wants to have available concurrently. The data in these spreadsheets may be linked or entirely separate, and they may or may not be displayed in a three-dimensional (3-D) image.

The sections of the chapter are as follows:

10.1 Styles for related spreadsheets
10.2 Linked spreadsheets
10.3 Designing linked spreadsheets
10.4 Designing three-dimensional spreadsheets
10.5 Guidelines for using multiple, linked, and 3-D spreadsheets

NOTE: While the examples used in this chapter are all built using *Lotus 1-2-3* Release 3, they apply equally well to any other spreadsheet program that supports linking. The exact technique of achieving linking may differ from program to program, but the concepts of linking, and the guidelines used to ensure good style apply in general.

10.1 STYLES FOR RELATED SPREADSHEETS

There are essentially three styles of setting up related spreadsheets.

- *Multiple spreadsheets in a single file.* These are two or more distinct spreadsheets with related data stored in a single file.

These spreadsheets must be loaded in RAM at the same time. There may or may not be linking between cells in the separate spreadsheets. If multiple spreadsheets are *not* linked, changes to one spreadsheet will not affect other spreadsheets. Storing information in a multiple spreadsheet file makes it easy to retrieve related information, even though the individual spreadsheets are not dependent on one another.

- *Linked spreadsheets.* A set of spreadsheets (or spreadsheet files) with related data, including cells in one spreadsheet that are automatically connected through cell references with cells in other spreadsheets in the set. Linked spreadsheets may have different formats. They may or may not be in memory together, but usually are. Some spreadsheet programs permit linking to spreadsheets on disk files. Spreadsheet linking is now a feature of several popular spreadsheet programs, including *Lotus 1-2-3* Release 3, *Microsoft Excel*, and *SuperCalc5*.

- *3-D spreadsheets.* A set of multiple spreadsheets having the identical row-and-column layout of information. In *Lotus 1-2-3* Release 3, these spreadsheets are treated as a group. The data are related, and the setup is referred to as three-dimensional or 3-D. If a row or column is inserted on one sheet, the same change in format is applied to all sheets in the set. Arithmetic operations can be performed across a row, down a column, or (in the third dimension) through related cells on the set of spreadsheets. There is usually linking between cells, but this is not mandatory.

The actual display of more than one spreadsheet on-screen is a separate matter. Depending on the software, the possibilities are:

- windowing
- perspective

Windowing. Individual spreadsheets occupy different areas of the screen without overlap. These areas are called *windows*. *Microsoft Excel* can display spreadsheets in windows.

Perspective. The screen is split into equal overlapping areas so that several spreadsheets may be displayed in perspective. *Lotus 1-2-3* Release 3 and *SuperCalc5* can display spreadsheets in perspective, and descriptions of these programs sometimes refer to this display feature as "3-D."

10.2 LINKED SPREADSHEETS

In spreadsheet linking, two or more spreadsheets are loaded into RAM. The user can work with each spreadsheet independently, or treat the spreadsheets as an interdependent set. In the latter case, the contents of one spreadsheet can depend on the values or results in other spreadsheets. Thus, several spreadsheets can be linked so that changes made to one spreadsheet are automatically reflected in other spreadsheets that are linked to it.

The benefits of linking spreadsheets are that individual spreadsheets can be kept smaller, more specific, and more manageable. Together, the linked spreadsheets can contain a large amount of information that can be automatically summarized or consolidated.

The concept of linking information from one spreadsheet to another is a natural one in the business context. If you open any multipaged financial report, for example, you will find that information is often carried forward and backward across pages. This is another form of linking.

Modular design. Linking spreadsheets permits modular design. For example, instead of storing the detailed expenses of five departments of a company on one large, unwieldy spreadsheet, five separate spreadsheets can store the expenses for the departments, and a linkage can be established to a sixth spreadsheet that consolidates the information for all departments. Thus, changes made to one department spreadsheet are automatically reflected in the consolidated spreadsheet for the company.

Economy of processing. Another advantage of linked spreadsheets is that by storing information in individual (and smaller) spreadsheets, the processing time required for any changes is significantly less than if the changes have to be made to a very large spreadsheet.

10.3 DESIGNING LINKED SPREADSHEETS

There are two ways spreadsheets can be linked. This section describes a general style of linking. A variant of this style, the 3-D spreadsheet, is described in Section 10.4.

The general style of linking permits information in any cell or range of cells of a spreadsheet to be linked to any cells of another spreadsheet. There is no restriction on the shape and format of each spreadsheet. Operations performed on one spreadsheet (such

FIGURE 10–1 Linked Spreadsheets

BALANCE.WK3:

A	A	B	C	D
11				
12	STOCKHOLDERS' EQUITY			
13	Common shares	1500000		
14	Preferred shares	680000		
15	Retained earnings	450000+<<C:\DATA\INCOME.WK3>>A:B10..A:B10		
16		--------		

INCOME.WK3 (stored in the directory C:\DATA):

A	A		B	C
6	Revenue	120000		
7				
8	Expenses	89000		
9		-------		
10	Net income	+B6-B8		
11		=======		

as inserting or deleting rows or columns, or formatting of cell ranges), do *not* affect the linked spreadsheets.

Example.

Figure 10–1 shows two linked spreadsheets. The formulas are shown to illustrate how the spreadsheets are linked. The BALANCE.WK3 spreadsheet contains the balance sheet, with only the Stockholders' Equity shown. For illustrative purposes, the spreadsheet INCOME.WK3 contains a simplified version of the complete income statement.

Note that the formula in cell B15 (Retained earnings) of the BALANCE.WK3 spreadsheet is linked to cell B10 (Net income) of the spreadsheet INCOME.WK3. In Release 3 of *Lotus 1-2-3* (used for this example), a spreadsheet is referenced by its filename as well as by a sheet identification. The top sheet of a spreadsheet (even if there is only one sheet) is identified as Sheet A. Thus, to refer to cell B10 of the spreadsheet INCOME.WK3 stored in the directory DATA in drive C, the specification of the link is

<<C:\DATA\INCOME.WK3>>A:B10..A:B10

Rules of Style

The following seven rules of style are recommended for the design of linked spreadsheets:

1. Link spreadsheets only if linking simplifies the design and makes the spreadsheets easier to maintain.

2. In the documentation block of a spreadsheet, show:

   - A list of all linked spreadsheets. The reader or user is thus explicitly informed of cell and spreadsheet relationships.

   - A comment as to whether the spreadsheets are linked to form a 3-D spreadsheet.

3. Include the names and the directory of the linked spreadsheets in all affected spreadsheets.

   Example. If spreadsheet A is linked to spreadsheets B and C, then the documentation in spreadsheet A should state this fact. The documentation in spreadsheet B should state the link with A, as should the documentation in spreadsheet C. There is no link between B and C, and this need not be mentioned in either spreadsheet B or C documentation.

4. Document the details of each link, either by explanatory notes placed in adjacent cells, or a cell noting facility. Also identify the purpose of the link. (See also Chapter 6 on documenting cell contents.)

   Example. The following cell note explains the link between the retained earnings amount in a balance sheet and an income statement, each stored in separate *Lotus 1-2-3* Release 3 spreadsheets:

   > The 1990 year-end retained earnings amount is calculated by adding the net income amount in cell B10 of the spreadsheet INCOME.WK3 to the opening retained earnings amount in cell B15 on this spreadsheet.

5. When one spreadsheet with external links is loaded, some spreadsheet programs load all linked spreadsheets automatically. Other programs rely on the user to load the linked spreadsheets individually, in the proper sequence. In the latter case, if the loading sequence is incorrect, or if

one of the linked spreadsheets is not loaded, the results in the other linked spreadsheets may be erroneous. To avoid this pitfall, load and save linked spreadsheets as a group, if possible. Spreadsheet programs have different names for these groups. For instance, in *Lotus 1-2-3* Release 3, these spreadsheets should be part of the same file. In *Microsoft Excel*, the spreadsheets would be saved as a "workspace."

6. Use the cell protection feature on the formulas that establish the linking, so that changes to such links will not be accidental. The linking relationships can be quite complicated, and inadvertent changes to these relationships can ruin the accuracy of your model. (See Section 6.5 on protecting cell contents.)

7. File the hard copy formula printouts of linked spreadsheets together. Similarly, perform backup of linked spreadsheets as a group. Backing up single spreadsheets without backing up the linked spreadsheets is risky.

10.4 DESIGNING THREE-DIMENSIONAL SPREADSHEETS

A three-dimensional spreadsheet is a group of several spreadsheets that have a common size, shape, and format. Operations performed on one spreadsheet (such as the insertion or deletion of rows or columns), automatically affect the size and shape of all other spreadsheets in the 3-D group (called *Group* mode in Release 3). Changing the format (for instance, decimal to percent) of any cells on one spreadsheet automatically changes the format of the corresponding cells on all other spreadsheets in the group.

Example 1.

Figure 10–2 is a 3-D spreadsheet. The BUDGET.WK3 spreadsheet has three component sheets: Sheet A is the consolidated cash budget, Sheet B is the cash budget for Sales Department A, and Sheet C is the cash budget for Sales Department B. The value in each cell in Sheet A is the sum of the corresponding cells in Sheets B and C. Thus, the formula in cell B13 (Accounts Receivable, Jan/90) in Sheet A reads:

@SUM(B:B13..C:B13)

Similarly, the formula in cell C13 in Sheet A reads:

@SUM(B:C13..C:C13)

FIGURE 10–2 Three-Dimensional Spreadsheet

Sheet A of BUDGET.WK3

A	A	B	C
7	All American Sporting Goods		
8	Consolidated Cash Budget		
9	For the Fiscal Year to Dec 31, 1990		
10			
11	Jan/90	Feb/90	Mar/90
12	Cash Receipts:		
13	Accounts receivable	$150,000	$178,000	$200,000
14	Interest	35,000	20,000	42,000
15	Other sources	5,500	6,500	4,600
16		--------	--------	--------
17	Total cash receipts	$190,500	$204,500	$246,600

Sheet B of BUDGET.WK3

B	A	B	C
7	All American Sporting Goods		
8	Cash Budget, Sales Department A		
9	For the Fiscal Year to Dec 31, 1990		
10			
11	Jan/90	Feb/90	Mar/90
12	Cash Receipts:		
13	Accounts receivable	$100,000	$118,000	$125,000
14	Interest	20,000	15,000	32,000
15	Other sources	5,000	3,500	3,600
16		--------	--------	--------
17	Total cash receipts	$125,000	$136,500	$160,600

Sheet C of BUDGET.WK3

C	A	B	C
7	All American Sporting Goods		
8	Cash Budget, Sales Department B		
9	For the Fiscal Year to Dec 31, 1990		
10			
11	Jan/90	Feb/90	Mar/90
12	Cash Receipts:		
13	Accounts receivable	$50,000	$60,000	$75,000
14	Interest	15,000	5,000	10,000
15	Other sources	500	3,000	1,000
16		--------	--------	-------
17	Total cash receipts	$65,500	$68,000	$86,000

Notice that the three sheets are identical in size, shape, and format. Changes made to any of the numbers in Sheets B and C are automatically reflected in Sheet A.

Three-dimensional spreadsheets are particularly suitable for use in situations where (a) there is uniformity in the meaning of the columns and rows between the spreadsheets, and (b) there are three dimensions in the data.

Example 2.

In a 3-D spreadsheet, rows are used to hold income and expense information, columns are used to hold information for each month, and each individual spreadsheet represents an individual department. For the 3-D spreadsheet shown in Figure 10-2, if column C on one spreadsheet is used to hold data for February 1990, then all column Cs in all the linked spreadsheets must also hold information for February 1990, although for different departments.

In determining which information to place in each dimension of the 3-D spreadsheet, use the rows and columns to represent the most commonly needed information and the data that must be viewed as a unit.

Example 3.

A 3-D spreadsheet is designed for budget planning, where each department prepares a 12-month detailed budget. The rows and columns should be used to hold 12 months of information for each department spreadsheet. The third dimension represents the separate departments.

In a comparative income statement, the performance of departments is compared on a month-to-month basis. It may be appropriate to design a 3-D spreadsheet such that the income and expense items form the rows and the departments form columns, with each spreadsheet representing the information for the individual months.

10.5 GUIDELINES FOR USING MULTIPLE, LINKED, AND 3-D SPREADSHEETS

- Use a standard two-dimensional style of spreadsheet whenever the model can easily be accommodated and managed. Single-page spreadsheets have the merits of simplicity and unity, as long as their capacity for displaying information is not unduly stretched.

- When a spreadsheet model contains several large components, consider splitting the model into several pages or sheets.

- If information from one or more spreadsheets is to be carried forward, transferred, summarized, or consolidated on another spreadsheet, consider linking the spreadsheets. Spreadsheets should only be linked if this style simplifies the design and renders the spreadsheets easier to maintain.

- If information on two or more related spreadsheets is in identical form and layout, consider the use of a 3-D spreadsheet.

- Never organize several spreadsheets into a 3-D spreadsheet if there are major differences in the format and contents of the spreadsheets. For such spreadsheets, it is better to link them.

CHAPTER ELEVEN

Style for Spreadsheet Databases

Most spreadsheet programs provide some means of setting up and manipulating a database. A *database* is any collection of information organized in a systematic and consistent manner, usually for a specific purpose. For example, an inventory list is a database set up to track items stored in a warehouse; a library catalog is a database designed for the orderly storage and retrieval of publications in a library system. While larger databases are often more effectively set up on database management programs such as *dBASE III PLUS* or *dBASE IV*, it is quite common business practice to use a spreadsheet or integrated programs for limited amounts of database work.

This chapter establishes guidelines for the use and operation of a database implemented on a spreadsheet. The material is organized as follows:

11.1 Database terms and concepts
11.2 When to use a spreadsheet database
11.3 Guidelines for designing a spreadsheet database
11.4 Guidelines for database operations

11.1 DATABASE TERMS AND CONCEPTS

A spreadsheet database is organized as a range of adjacent rows and columns. Each row makes up a *record* of the database, while each column holds information on a category of data, called a *field*, for all records. Most spreadsheet programs require that each column be headed by a *field name*. For the database to work

FIGURE 11–1 Employee Database on a Spreadsheet

	A	B	C	D	E	F
5			All American Sporting Goods			
6			Employee Database			
7						
8	STAFFID	LASTNAME	FIRSTNAME	TITLE	DEPARTMENT	SALARY
9	314583	Alenzo	Nina	Manager	Data Center	$45,500
10	364781	Ballentine	Rosaline	V.P.	Sales	$76,900
11	234154	Ferguson	Joseph	Operator	Data Center	$21,700
12	323542	Fung	Amy	Analyst	Data Center	$32,000
13	215163	Gonzo	Allan	Analyst	Finance	$34,500
14	356713	Jones	Stanley	Salesagent	Sales	$36,800
15	432641	Masako	Mary	Secretary	Sales	$19,700
16	234145	Molina	Angela	Clerk	Accounting	$18,900
17	241555	Baloney	Brian	Buyer	Sales	$28,000
18	312615	Peckford	John	Receiver	Warehouse	$18,500
19	237187	Peterson	Kenneth	Shipper	Warehouse	$20,500
20	345136	Powell	William	V.P.	Data Center	$68,900
21	315612	Singh	Gudel	Salesagent	Sales	$39,000
22	310231	Smith	Gary	Manager	Finance	$43,500
23	344131	Wang	Lynda	Controller	Accounting	$42,800

properly, there must be consistency in the content and style of all the information contained in the database.

Typical operations with spreadsheet databases include recording, sorting, searching, selecting, extracting, summarizing, and reporting. In sorting operations, the user must specify one or more *keys* or key fields to be used to establish the order in which the data is to be sequenced. In data selecting and extracting operations, a *criterion* or *criteria* must be specified to instruct the program how to identify the required records.

Example.

Figure 11–1 is part of a *Lotus 1-2-3* spreadsheet showing an employee database for All American Sporting Goods Ltd. The database contains 15 records in rows 9 to 23; row 8 contains the field names. The information for each record is entered in six data fields (columns A to F). Notice the consistency of content and style. For instance:

- The field names are all written as one word and capitalized; they do not contain hyphens or periods.

- Column A is the Staff ID field and contains only the six-digit identification number of the employee.

- Columns B and C contain the last name and first name of the employee, consistently in that order and with no middle initials.

- Column D is the Title field. Note that the titles of salesagent (all one word) and V.P. (standard abbreviation with periods) are entered in exactly the same style. Similar consistency is observed for the field of Department.

- Column F contains the salaries, formatted to consistently display the dollar sign ($) with commas at the thousands.

These elements of style are most important for database operations such as sorting and retrieval. If the database is not standardized in this way, it is quite likely that the sort or retrieve commands could produce erroneous output.

11.2 WHEN TO USE A SPREADSHEET DATABASE

The following considerations may help to determine whether a database should be implemented on a spreadsheet or on a database management program:

Ease of use. Spreadsheets provide a relatively easy means of working with databases. Database layout on a spreadsheet is very straightforward, with columns for the data fields and rows for the records. The user can often view database records at a glance, or browse with the cursor. There are only a few new commands to learn.

Quick implementation. Implementing a database on a spreadsheet can be as simple as typing in the data records. There is no need to learn new methods of entering data. The user can correct mistakes quickly on a cell-by-cell basis.

Ability to customize. The macro facilities of the spreadsheet program are available for customizing database operations. However, spreadsheet programs offer limited capabilities for extracting data and formatting the output in different styles of report. It is very difficult, for instance, to format mailing lists, form letters, invoices, and summary tables from spreadsheet databases. If reporting requirements are complicated, it may be better to turn to a database program with greater capacity and flexibility in report formats.

Memory and spreadsheet size. Most spreadsheet programs require that the entire database reside in computer memory while it is being worked with. Consequently, if a database contains a large number of records, it might be too big for a spreadsheet program to handle, and a database management program might be more suitable. The number of records that can be kept on a spreadsheet database depends on the maximum size of the spreadsheet, which in turn depends on the amount of computer memory available.

Query capabilities. Spreadsheet programs are ideal for simple query commands. Where complex queries are needed, database management programs may be more suitable. So look ahead to the types of queries you anticipate doing on the database, and decide whether the spreadsheet program is capable of meeting your needs.

Sorting capabilities. Sorting using spreadsheet programs usually requires very simple commands. Note that some spreadsheet programs offer only limited sorting of databases. For example, *Lotus 1-2-3* Release 2.01 only permits two sort keys, and *Microsoft Excel* only three, although *Lotus 1-2-3* Release 3 supports 255 sort keys. Where complex sorting and the use of many sort keys is required, a spreadsheet model may not be appropriate.

11.3 GUIDELINES FOR DESIGNING A SPREADSHEET DATABASE

If a spreadsheet is appropriate for a database, here are ten guidelines for the design process.

1. *Determine what information is to constitute the records, and select headings for the data fields.* Records must be placed in rows, while the data fields must occupy the columns.

   Example. In the case of the employee database in Figure 11–1, the employees are represented in the database as records, while the separate items of data about each employee form the data fields.

2. *Format each data field consistently.* For example, column C in Figure 11–1 is used to hold first names. Initials should not be placed in this data field.

3. *Standardize the coding of text and data in each field.* For example, column E in Figure 11–1 contains the names of

departments, and they must be consistently spelled. Thus, for the accounting department, you should always enter the department name as "Accounting" (capitalized A, followed by a full spelling of the rest of the word), as opposed to a variety of different spellings (such as "accounting," "Acctng," or "Acct"). This is very important because the field contents affect the sorting of the database, as well as database query and extraction operations.

4. *Use self-evident field names.* Each field in the database must be headed by a field name so that the intended content of any field is clear. The field names should be concise and self-evident. Where there may be misunderstanding on the intent of a particular data field, use cell notes or include information in the documentation section of the spreadsheet. (See Chapter 6 on documenting cell contents.)

5. *Field names must be unique.* The same field name cannot be used for two different data fields. Otherwise, erroneous output will be the result. Use unique data field names to avoid confusing the reader, as well as the spreadsheet program itself. That is, do not head two columns with the same label. Where abbreviations are used, standardize the shorter forms.

6. *Format the cells in a data field in a consistent manner.* For example, the data field headed "salaries" should contain dollar amounts with two places of decimal accuracy.

7. *If more data may be added to the database, position the database block with care.* The database block should be located on the spreadsheet so that adding records does not affect the operations of the entire spreadsheet. For instance, if there are macros, place the macro block above or to the right of the database, not below the database. If the macros are placed below, the database may "grow" into the area containing the macros. (See also Chapter 3 on block design, and Section 4.5 on the macro block.)

8. *Clearly identify the input block, the output block, and the criterion block* by labeling these blocks, or including their locations in the documentation. Named ranges can be used effectively to identify these blocks. For example, you can name the input block as INPUT, the output block

as OUTPUT, and the criterion block as CRITERION, assuming that only one block is used for each input, output, and criterion in the spreadsheet. For a work group, standardize naming conventions and the amount and style of documentation.

9. *Where the criterion is specified as a logical comparison, include the correct data field label in the criterion block,* even though the spreadsheet program may not use this cell to perform the data extraction operation. The inclusion of the data field label enables the user to more readily identify the data management operation.

10. *For more advanced operations,* consider using macros to ensure consistent and error-free operations. (See also Chapter 9 on macros and menus.)

11.4 GUIDELINES FOR DATABASE OPERATIONS

Two main types of database operations are typically implemented on a spreadsheet. The first type includes data management commands such as sorting, query, and record extraction, each of which is performed using spreadsheet commands (e.g., **/Data Sort** or **/Data Query** in *Lotus 1-2-3*). The second type includes statistical database functions, performed using built-in spreadsheet functions such as @DSUM.

Data management commands. The most commonly performed data management operation is to sort the database on one or more key data fields. Data query and data extract are other commonly performed database operations. While the sorting of databases is straightforward and requires no standardization, the use of data query and data extract can better be accomplished if a consistent style is adopted.

Most spreadsheet programs require that the input block, the output block, and the criterion block be specified to the data management command before data query or extraction can be performed. The input block specifies the cells containing the database, the output block specifies the cells to contain the output from the data extract command, and the criterion block specifies the cells containing the data selection criteria.

Example.
In Figure 11–1, to extract the records of all employees working in the EDP center, we specify the input block as cells A8..G23. The cri-

terion appears in cells H2 and H3, with cell H2 specifying the data field for selection, and cell H3 specifying the value in the data field that meets the selection criteria:

```
   H
2  Department
3  EDP Center
```

We set up an output block in cells H8..K8, containing the data fields: Lastname, Firstname, Title, and Salary. The data extraction will result in the following output:

```
    H         I          J          K
8   Lastname  Firstname  Title      Salary
9   Alenzo    Nina       Manager    $45,500
10  Ferguson  Joseph     Operator   $21,700
11  Fung      Amy        Analyst    $32,000
12  Powell    William    V.P.       $68,900
```

Statistical database functions. These are built-in spreadsheet functions designed to perform statistical calculations on database data. Unlike a statistical function that works with a cell range, a database statistical function requires the specification of an input block, an offset, and a criterion block. For example, the following function calculates the average salaries for the EDP Center:

```
DAVG(A8..G23,6,H2..H3)
```

where A8..G23 is the input block, 6 is the offset, and H2..H3 is the criterion block. Cells H2 and H3 contain the following criterion:

```
   H
2  Department
3  EDP Center
```

yielding the average salary of $42,025 for the EDP Center.

CHAPTER TWELVE

Style for Spreadsheet Graphics

This chapter explains the main points of style for graphics created from spreadsheet data. (We use the term graphics to include all types of graphs, charts, or similar visual presentations of data.) The chapter includes an overview of common types of graphics and their uses, as well as some guidelines for linking spreadsheet data to graphics.

The topics included in this chapter are:

12.1 Hardware and operating requirements
12.2 Software options
12.3 Types of graphics
12.4 Three-dimensional graphics
12.5 Standard graphic components
12.6 Guidelines for graphic style
12.7 Guidelines in designing spreadsheets for graphics

Most spreadsheet programs provide a means of presenting spreadsheet data in graphic form; alternatively, a user can turn to specialized graphics software for this purpose. This style of information is often most suited to analysis or presentation to a business audience. Visual summaries are increasingly common in industry, government, research, and mass media or consumer-oriented presentations. Computer-generated graphics can be reproduced in a variety of attractive formats, including black and white or color printouts, overhead projection transparencies, slides, and either free-running or manually controlled screenshows on desktop monitors or large screens.

12.1 HARDWARE AND OPERATING REQUIREMENTS

The minimum hardware and operating requirements for using a graphics program are

- A Hercules, MCGA, CGA, EGA, or VGA graphics adapter card.

- A graphics monitor that is compatible with the graphics adapter card.

- A printer with graphics capability, supported by the graphics program; dot matrix is suitable for draft output, but a laser printer is required for presentation quality. Examples in this chapter were developed with *SuperCalc4, SuperCalc5,* and *Lotus 1-2-3* Release 3. Some printouts were done on a standard laser printer, others on a dot matrix printer; the difference in quality is quite evident.

12.2 SOFTWARE OPTIONS

To produce graphics, the user may select from several types of software.

- Graphics software that is fully integrated with a spreadsheet program (such as *Framework III, Symphony, Microsoft Excel, SuperCalc5,* or *Lotus 1-2-3* Release 3). Fully integrated in this sense means that the user can create the graphic directly from within the spreadsheet program, and can link the data to the graph so that one is automatically updated from the other.

- A partly integrated graphics program such as the PrintGraph program in *Lotus 1-2-3* Releases 2.01 and 2.2. To print a graph, you must first save the graph in a .PIC file, then use the PrintGraph program to print the .PIC file.

- Standalone graphics programs such as *Harvard Graphics* or *Microsoft Chart.* These provide the advantage of a very large range of graphic functions that enables more fine-tuning of visual presentation style.

- A small range of RAM-resident utilities such as *Graph-in-the-Box*, from New England Software.

The remaining sections of this chapter are concerned with style considerations when transforming spreadsheet data into graphics.

12.3 TYPES OF GRAPHICS

The choice of a graphic type is very important, and the characteristics of the graphic should be well suited to the nature of the data and to the purpose of the visual presentation. Presenting information by using an inappropriate kind of graph can confuse, rather than clarify.

The names of graphics types may vary slightly from program to program. The terms *graph* and *chart* are quite often used interchangeably. The standard types are

- Pie

- Bar

- Stacked bar

- Line

- Area

- Mixed bar and line

- X-Y

- Hi-lo

The main characteristics of each of these types are as follows.

Pie Chart

A pie chart is created using the values for a single data variable. Each value is represented by a segment (slice) of a circle (pie). The graphics program routinely converts each value into a percentage, and the percentages add up to 100.

Best uses. Pie charts are best suited for visual display of how parts relate to a whole. They are especially effective for comparisons of percentages. For broader comparisons that include another variable, several pie charts could be used. For example, the components of a firm's expenses for two consecutive years could be presented in two separate pie charts.

FIGURE 12–1   Simple Pie Chart

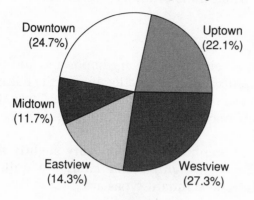

EasyRider CarSales Inc.
April Sales: Chrysler Magic Wagons

Downtown (24.7%)

Uptown (22.1%)

Midtown (11.7%)

Eastview (14.3%)

Westview (27.3%)

Total Units Sold: 77

Avoid pie charts when more than five or six segments are to be displayed. Use colors, hatching or shading conservatively to distinguish pie slices. If two or more data variables are to be plotted, consider using a bar, stacked bar, or line graph.

Example.
A pie chart could show the percentage contributions of several sources of cash to total cash inflow for a fiscal period. Another chart could show the proportion of expenses allotted to different categories of spending. Figure 12–1 is a pie chart showing the contribution of each of five dealers to a company's total sales of Chrysler Magic Wagons for a particular month.

Variants.   An *exploded pie* chart provides for one or more segments to be visually pulled away from the other segments, for emphasis. Figure 12–2 shows a pie chart with two segments exploded.

Bar Graph

A bar graph typically displays information in the form of vertical bars arranged side by side for comparison. Each value of a variable is shown as a vertical bar with its base on the horizontal axis. When two or more variables are to be displayed, each variable is shown by a separate bar, usually distinguished by hatches, colors, or shading.

Best uses. Although a bar chart can be used to display a single data variable, it is best suited for visual comparison of several data variables. To avoid clutter, show less than five variables. For more than five variables, consider combining some variables or breaking up the exhibit into several graphics, each emphasizing a different aspect of the data. (See also the section on line graphs later in this chapter.)

Example.
A bar graph is ideal for comparing the sales figures of several dealers over several months, or the production of a number of commodities by several countries (states, provinces, or regions) in a single period. Figure 12–3 is a bar graph showing the sale of Magic Wagons by two dealers over four months.

Variants. Bar graphs may also be called *column charts*, or *horizontal bar charts*, depending on whether they are vertical or horizontal. Another variant is the *paired* or *clustered bar graph*, which displays pairs or clusters of bars side by side. For instance, comparisons of total dollar sales in four branches for each of 12 months would be shown by 12 clusters of four bars. A *histogram* is another special kind of bar graph that is used to show frequencies or statistical distributions. (See also "stacked bar", in the following section.) Figure 12–4 is a horizontal bar graph illustrating the effective use of the left axis for place name labels and the use of data-labels for the columns to show precise dollar amounts raised. This graph conveys both absolute and relative data without complexity.

Stacked Bar Graph

In a stacked bar graph, instead of displaying the data variables in side-by-side bars, you show them one on top of the other in stacks. Stacked bars combine the display features of pie charts and bar graphs. That is, you can see the contribution made by any component to the complete stack, and you can compare one stack with another. Shading, hatching, or color can be used effectively.

Variants. The *100% chart* is structured and labeled to show the percentage contribution of each part of the stack to the whole.

FIGURE 12–2 Exploded Pie Chart

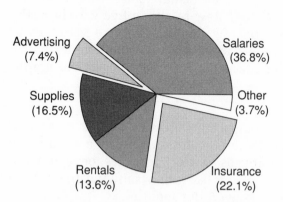

Glinert White Water Adventures
Operating Expenses 1990

Advertising
(7.4%)

Salaries
(36.8%)

Supplies
(16.5%)

Other
(3.7%)

Rentals
(13.6%)

Insurance
(22.1%)

Total Operating Expenses: $272,000

FIGURE 12–3 Simple Bar Graph

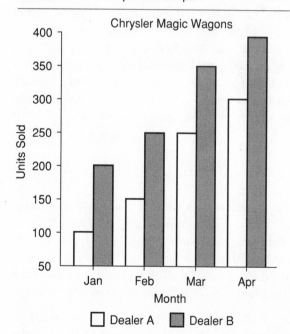

Chrysler Magic Wagons

□ Dealer A ▨ Dealer B

FIGURE 12–4 Horizontal Bar Graph

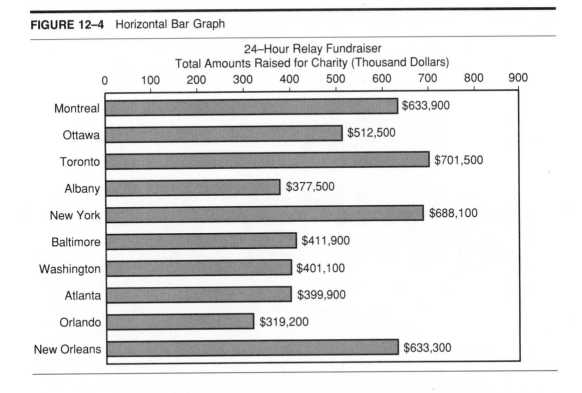

Best uses. Consider stacked bar when you need to (1) display how the data variables relate to others within the stack, and (2) compare the stacks of data variables with other stacks. The stacked bar can be quite effective in showing fluctuations in the components of a total from one category or period to another.

Example.

Figure 12–5 is a stacked bar graph showing the performance of two dealers and their sales of Magic Wagons over a four-month period. The graphs can show the trend of sales of each dealer, as well as the contribution to total sales by each dealer.

Line Graph

In a line graph, the values of each data variable are joined together by a line. There is a separate line for each variable. The lines make it easier to compare the trend of variables. This is sometimes called a *trend line graph*. Time is usually shown along the horizontal scale.

FIGURE 12–5 Stacked Bar Graph

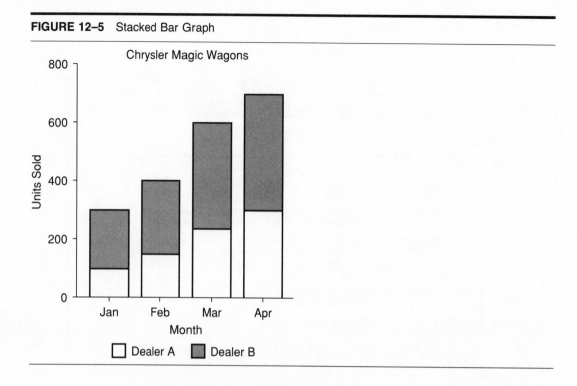

Best uses. Line graphs are ideal for presenting trends. Although bar graphs may also convey information on trends, line graphs are more effective. Line graphs are more suitable than bar graphs for continuous data variables. Bar graphs are more suitable for discrete data variables, or categories.

Variants. Two line graphs with different vertical scales, but a common (time) horizontal scale, could be shown on the same graphic. This type may be called a *multiple scale chart* or *dual Y-axis chart.* (See the description of "Mixed bar and line graph," later in this chapter, for precautions about scales.)

Example.

Figure 12–6 shows a line graph comparing the performance of two dealers over a four-month period.

Area Graph

An area graph looks like a line graph, but its lines are stacked vertically on a cumulative basis, just like a stacked bar graph, and

FIGURE 12–6 Line Graph

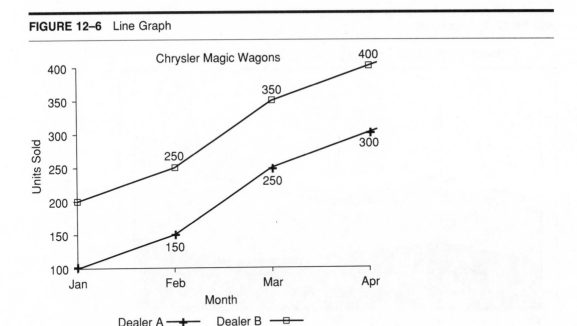

the areas between the lines are filled in with different colors or shading, preferably with the darkest tones at the bottom. Thus, the area graph has a multilayered aspect. Time is usually the horizontal axis.

Best uses. An area graph can depict a trend, as well as show the relative importance of several components at each time period. Area graphs should be used for continuous data. Sometimes, the shading of the area will make it impossible to see the exact data points on the line. This may be partly offset by using a grid.

Variants. If the upper line represents 100 percent, then each lower line represents components of the whole.

Example.

Figure 12–7 is an area graph showing the performance of three groups of subsidiary companies over a five-year period. The Y-axis on the right is used for the scale, and a vertical grid has been added to improve readability. The upper line shows the cumulative total for the three subsidiaries.

FIGURE 12–7 Area Graph

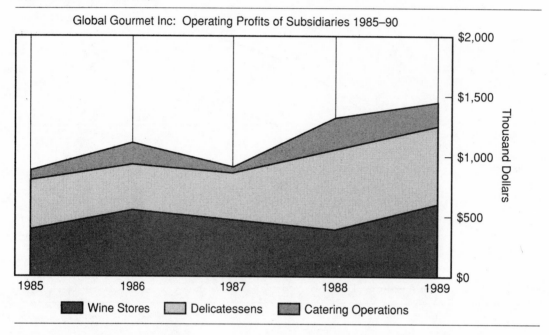

Global Gourmet Inc: Operating Profits of Subsidiaries 1985–90

Wine Stores   Delicatessens   Catering Operations

Mixed Bar and Line Graph

Within the same graphic, a mix of bar and line graphs may be used. This may also be called a *combination chart* or an *overlay*. Typically, bars represent one type of data series, and lines represent another type. Two different vertical scales are necessary, one for the bars (usually on the left axis) and one for the lines (usually the right axis). Both scales must be clearly labeled to avoid confusion between them. There will also be a horizontal axis, also with its label. Make sure that the units of each scale are shown. A mixed graph should probably not contain more than one data series for each type of graphic; otherwise, the message of the graphic can be lost in its own complexity.

Example.

Figure 12–8 is a mixed graph showing total sales as a bar graph and operating profits as a line graph over a five-year period. The graph indicates a relationship between sales and profits, as well as the trend of business over time. Note the use of the two Y-axes and the respective scale indicators to clarify what each part of the graph is showing. A horizontal grid has been added for each scale,

FIGURE 12–8 Mixed Graph

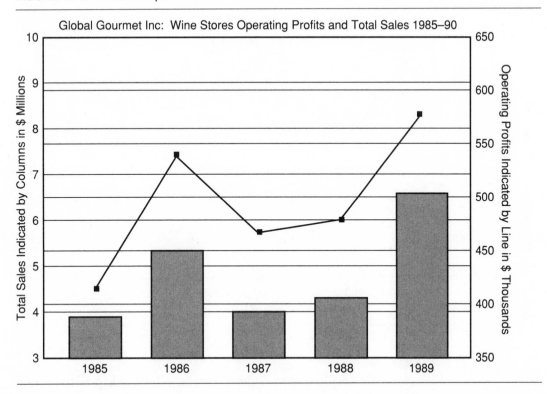

Global Gourmet Inc: Wine Stores Operating Profits and Total Sales 1985–90

X-Y Graph

and the shading of the bars has been kept at a subdued level to achieve visual balance. The X-Y graph is also known as a *scatter chart*, *scattergram*, or *scatterplot*. The X-Y graph is used to display the correlation between two data variables, an X value and a Y value. The way in which the data points scatter or cluster on the graph indicates the degree and type of relationship between the two variables. It is generally not good form to use time as a variable.

Variants. Rarely in spreadsheet programs, but commonly in statistical programs, it is possible to plot a trend line that represents the general direction and shape of the correlation between two variables. This is known as a *regression line*.

Best uses. The X-Y graph should be used to graphically analyze the relationships between two variables.

FIGURE 12–9   X-Y Graph

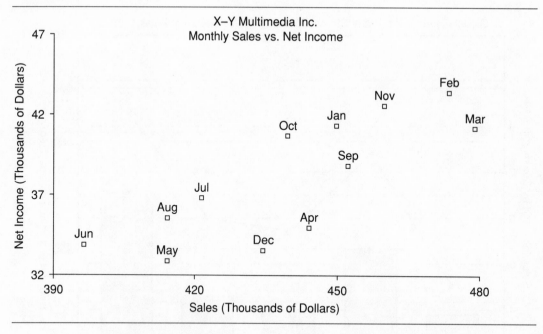

Example.

Figure 12–9 is an X-Y graph showing the relationship between net income and sales for the months of January to June.

Hi-Lo Graph

A hi-lo graph plots the high and low values of data variables. Most hi-lo graphs can also plot data values in between the high and low values.

Variants.   A common variant is the HLCO (High-Low-Close-Open) graph, which plots the high and low prices of several stocks for each day, over a week's time, as well as the open and close prices for each day. Other applications include the graphing of fluctuations in exchange rates, or of the high and low daily temperatures over a period of time. Sometimes a bar graph and a moving-average line are added to the lower half of the HLCO graph.

Example.

Figure 12–10 is a hi-lo graph of a stock's performance over the period of a week.

FIGURE 12–10 Hi-Lo Graph

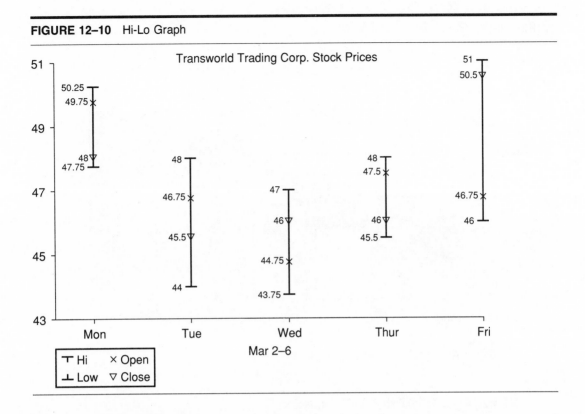

12.4 THREE-DIMENSIONAL GRAPHICS

Some spreadsheet programs can display certain graph types in three-dimensional style.

Example.

Figure 12–11 is a three-dimensional bar graph that presents the same information as shown in the two-dimensional bar graph of Figure 12–3. While three-dimensional graphs may initially be impressive to look at, they rarely add any information to what you would see in a standard two-dimensional graph. Many people find three-dimensional graphs confusing to read and interpret.

Pie charts and area graphs adapt most easily to three-dimensional form; column and bar graphs in 3-D may also be effective. Line, X-Y, and Hi-Lo do not benefit from the third dimension. The most important consideration in selecting graphic features is that the medium should enhance and not overwhelm the message.

FIGURE 12–11 Three-Dimensional Bar Graph

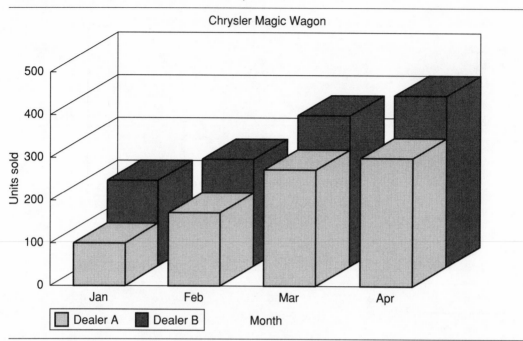

12.5 STANDARD GRAPHIC COMPONENTS

A number of stylistic components have become standard in the effective presentation of graphic information. Most of them are generally accepted conventions for graphics in any kind of publishing and are not peculiar to spreadsheet graphics. In integrated spreadsheet programs, each graph type is set up to provide a default style of labels, markings, and colors or shading. To these, one or more of the components shown in Table 12–1 may be added.

12.6 GUIDELINES FOR GRAPHIC STYLE

Ten guidelines for using graphics generated from spreadsheets are as follows.

1. *Clearly define the purpose of the graphic.* This purpose must be clear to the reader, and the information presented should be self-explanatory.

2. *Keep it simple.* A cluttered graphic is worse than none at all. You can achieve visual impact more easily with

TABLE 12-1 Standard Graphic Components

Axes	Most graphics have one (horizontal) X-axis, and one (vertical, left) Y-axis. Conventionally, the X-axis indicates time periods, data categories, or independent variables; the Y-axis indicates amounts, quantities, or a dependent variable. Both axes must have labels, and units of measurement, currency, time, etc. must also be stated. A second Y-axis may be added to the right bar graph.
Fill pattern	For the inside of bars, columns, pie slices, and area graphs, the fill pattern is typically solid, outline, or crosshatched in one of many possible ways. The legend should clearly indicate the desired interpretation meaning of the patterns.
Fill color	This is a standard way of differentiating elements of a graphic, such as pie slices, or parts of a stacked bar graph. Use bright colors for emphasis of a particular variable. Avoid putting red and green adjacent, because some people have trouble distinguishing these colors.
Fonts and text size	Consult the software manual to find out what fonts and sizes of text are available. Experiment to achieve the best visual balance and unity.
Footnotes or annotations	Some programs provide for brief comments of this type. Typically, they would appear below the main part of the graphic.
Format	Labels should be formatted consistently, either manually, or by a formatting feature on the program. Be consistent in format of dollar and other currency symbols, thousands commas, decimal places, integers, percentages in pie charts, and scientific notation such as exponents.
Frame style	Different frame styles may be available in some programs to enclose the area in which the graphic is printed.
Grid lines	These lines, drawn horizontally and/or vertically on the graphic, may help readability in some situations but be distracting in others. Tick marks may be better for some graphics.
Labels	A text word or phrase must be used to signify the meaning of axes, units, lines, bars, columns, or pie slices. Labels may also be used with specific data points, bars, or columns.

TABLE 12-1 (cont.)

Legend	This is a key or index to some identifying system of line drawing (e.g., continuous or broken), point marking (plus signs or small circles), fill patterns or color, used to indicate different data series in a graphic. It is not always required if the meaning is otherwise clear.
Line style	There may be a choice of solid, dotted, dashed, or no line to join data points. Symbols such as small squares may be used to indicate data points on the line. A solid line works well to emphasize one data series where several are shown on the same graphic. Projections of future trends are conventionally shown as dotted or dashed lines. Be careful to watch the balance of line style with the gridlines; it may be necessary to modify or cut the grid to keep a clean look. Do not join points that are not in sequence, such as in many X–Y graphs.
Scaling	It is essential that scales be the same when comparing two data series. Watch scales when doing overlays or printing graphs side by side. Scales are normally linear, that is, increasing in regular intervals. Manual scaling may be available to override default scales; this feature may also enable you to assign different values to the point of origin. *Logarithmic* and *semi-logarithmic* charts are variants of scaling, often used to depict rapidly rising rates of change, such as acceleration of a space vehicle or exponential growth of a population. These scales also make it easier to compare rates of change, as opposed to absolute amounts of change. The units used for any scale must always be indicated on the axis.
Tick mark	This is a small mark representing a value at a precise point on an axis. It may be possible to put tick marks inside or outside the axis line, or across it. Inside is generally preferred, but it is more important to maintain a consistent style from one axis to another. Tick marks can greatly improve the readability of a graphic. Sometimes grid lines are preferable.
Titles	A graphic should have a title that carries meaning. Split long titles into a main and "sub" on two lines. Titles are usually centered.

a single message than with an attempt to convey total information. Where there are several messages to get across, use a small set of simple graphics in preference to one huge, elaborate tapestry.

3. *Label graphics clearly.* The graphic should have a title, labels for the horizontal and vertical axes, labels for the tick marks on the axis, and a legend to indicate what each variable is. Check the spelling of all text, especially any in large type.

4. *Use fonts for visual impact.* If various fonts are available, use them for maximum visual impact. Use the same font for similar items in a graphic, but use different fonts to accentuate distinctions. Thus, labels for horizontal and vertical axes should be in the same font, but the main title of the graphic should be in a different, larger font.

5. *Use points of origin properly.* For example, in an area graph, you should never start the Y-axis at a non-zero point, because this distorts the visual relationship between the data variables.

6. *Use whole numbers for the scales.* It can be frustrating to try to interpret a graph with the axis marked off in uneven units. Set up tick marks at standard intervals such as 10, 20, 30, and so on, and not at 11.5, 21.5, 31.5, or the like. Whole numbers in standard intervals also make it easier to interpolate between scale values.

7. *Be careful with missing information.* For example, a pie chart must convey complete information. If there are missing values, a pie chart should either not be used, or if used, should clearly indicate that the values of some variables are missing.

8. *Keep fill patterns simple.* The "busier" the patterns, the harder it usually is for the reader to make distinctions between them. Some patterns may also distort, so check for this effect.

9. *Use contrasting colors.* The purpose of color in a graphic is to clarify distinctions. Be aware that some readers (about 4 percent) are colorblind and may not be able to distinguish between red and green. If in doubt, use fill patterns rather than colors.

10. *Choose the graph type carefully.* Know what types are suitable for different forms of data and different presentation purposes. Only use 3-D graphs, for instance, where they are clearly superior in terms of clarity of the message.

12.7 GUIDELINES IN DESIGNING SPREADSHEETS FOR GRAPHICS

Spreadsheet programs have different methods for transforming spreadsheet data into a graphic image. Nevertheless, there are some spreadsheet design guidelines you can follow to facilitate the creation of a graphic from the data.

- *Organize data in a logical manner that facilitates graph definitions.* For example, if a bar graph is to be created from a spreadsheet table, place the variables for each bar in adjoining rows and columns, in the same sequence as you want the bars to be displayed in the graph.

- *Label spreadsheet data clearly.* The X and Y axis labels should be included in the spreadsheet table. Usually, these labels should be the row and column headings of the data values. For example, in Figure 12–11, the numbers of Magic Wagons sold by Dealer A and Dealer B are clearly labeled; so are the months.

- *Give the spreadsheet a title that can also serve as the title or main heading of the graphic.* Keep the titles and labels short and descriptive. If the titles or labels are too long, they may clutter up the graphic and threaten its readability.

- *Format spreadsheet numbers for ease of presentation on the graphic.* For example, if you do not need to display up to two places of decimal in a graph, format the spreadsheet to the nearest whole numbers. Sometimes it is advisable to scale the numbers on the spreadsheet so that the values shown on the X or Y axis are in units of hundreds or thousands. This is particularly important if an automatic scaling feature is provided, because it could produce some unwanted results.

- *Document information about graphics on the spreadsheet itself.* Sufficient guidance should be provided for the user so that key elements of the design of the graphic are articulated. The information need not be very detailed.

Example.
Graph 1: Bar graph, months on the X-axis
Graph 2: Area graph, months on the X-axis
Graph 3: Pie chart, showing total for the year

CHAPTER THIRTEEN

Spreadsheet Printing and Publishing

This chapter presents guidelines and generally accepted standards of style for presenting spreadsheets in printed form. The material is divided into sections on:

13.1 Routine spreadsheet printing
13.2 Printing large spreadsheets
13.3 Sideways Landscape printing
13.4 Guidelines for sideways printing
13.5 Desktop publishing
13.6 Guidelines for desktop publishing

13.1 ROUTINE SPREADSHEET PRINTING

For routine spreadsheet printing, there are a number of basic style choices to be made:

- With or without borders (that is, the row numbers and column letters)

- With or without page numbers

- With or without headers or footers

- With or without a date stamp.

It may be advisable to standardize on some aspects of spreadsheet printing, especially where the output is shared with other members of a work group. Printing standards for an office can ensure that all spreadsheet printouts contain the information needed by others in the work group. The following guidelines are recommended.

- *Print with row-and-column borders* when users may need to identify cell addresses. It is essential to print the borders when spreadsheets are to show formulas.

- *Print without row-and-column borders* when cell addresses are not needed by users; for example, readers of financial statements, payment schedules, and so on. Omitting the borders fixes the reader's attention on the substance of the spreadsheet and its message.

- *Print page numbers* for spreadsheets that span several pages. Many spreadsheet programs enable you to specify automatic page numbering.

- *Use page headers and/or footers* when a spreadsheet consists of two or more pages. Some spreadsheet programs offer this feature; in other programs, you may have to improvise your own.

- *Use the date stamp* on each page of a multipage spreadsheet to ensure that each page represents the most current version, and that the pages will not be mixed up after printing. (See Chapter 4, Section 4.1 for use of the NOW function.)

13.2 PRINTING LARGE SPREADSHEETS

For a spreadsheet that contains too many columns to fit on a standard (8.5 in. by 11 in.) page, the choices are:

- *Print in a smaller font*, such as a 15- or 17-pitch condensed typeface. This method can be considered if the total width is under 132 characters for standard carriage printers, or under 230 characters for wide carriage printers. Most dot matrix printers are capable of compressed printing. Consult the printer manual to confirm this; consult the spreadsheet program manual for instructions on how to set up the printing options for compressed print. Figure 13–1 shows an example of a printer output set to 17 characters per inch compressed print.

- *Split the spreadsheet into several pages.* If the spreadsheet requires more space than the paper can hold, you may print the spreadsheet in parts, each part fitting onto a standard page.

FIGURE 13–1 Compressed Printer Output

Personal Net Worth and Estate Planning: Fiona W. Johnson   Date: 12-Jan-90

LIQUID ASSETS		SHORT-TERM LIABILITIES	
Checking account balance	2,445	Outstanding bills:	
Savings account balance	6,548	MasterCard	2,400
Certificate of deposit	3,000	American Express	1,540
Investment fund	45,000	Shell Oil	143
U.S. Govt Bonds	1,500	Sears	865
Stocks	6,580	Pacific Northwest Bell	60
Bonds	3,000	Seattle Power	125
	--------		--------
Total liquid assets	68,073	Total unpaid bills	5,133
NON-LIQUID ASSETS		LONG-TERM LIABILITIES	
House	180,000	Mortgage, house	120,000
Other real estate	78,000	Mortgage, real estate	60,000
Automobile	12,500	Car Loan	1,500
Jewelry	12,000		--------
	--------	Total long-term Liab.	181,500
Total non-liquid assets	282,500		
		OTHER LIABILITIES	
OTHER ASSETS		Stock margin account	4,000
Boat	45,000		--------
	--------	TOTAL LIABILITIES	190,633
TOTAL ASSETS	395,573	NET WORTH	204,940
	========		========

To view the entire spreadsheet, the pages have to be pasted together, which may not be satisfactory. It is also easy to mix up or misfile the pages of the printout.

- *Print the entire spreadsheet sideways or in landscape mode* (see Section 13.3).

13.3 SIDEWAYS (LANDSCAPE) PRINTING

Spreadsheets that take up many columns often cannot fit into a standard width page (8.5 in.). Printing the spreadsheet using the longer dimension of the page (11 in. or 14 in.) may solve the problem. Some spreadsheet programs such as *Lotus 1-2-3* Release 3 and *Microsoft Excel* can generate either vertical (portrait) or horizontal (landscape or "sideways") printouts. The printer in use must also have matching capability. However, software utility programs are also available for this purpose.

A sideways printing utility may be available in the main spreadsheet program, or you may consider an add-in program such as *Sideways* from Funk Software. These programs are straightforward to use, and they may offer a choice of fonts, even for a dot matrix printer.

Figure 13–2 is an example of the output from *Sideways*. Notice that we have used a small spreadsheet with only a few columns so that the example can fit into a printed page of the book. In practice, sideways printing is used when the spreadsheet has many columns that cannot be fitted on standard-size paper.

13.4 GUIDELINES FOR SIDEWAYS PRINTING

The following guidelines are recommended with respect to deciding when and how to use sideways printing.

- Where possible, avoid it. Generally, a spreadsheet should be printed on a single page, in the normal portrait mode. Use compressed printing if necessary, but watch its legibility.

- Consider splitting the spreadsheet into smaller components and providing the reader with a manageable series of smaller worksheets containing the same information. Print only one or two spreadsheets per page, by the normal method.

- If no other method works, use sideways printing. If the spreadsheet program does not provide a built-in sideways printing facility, use a reliable add-in program.

- For users in a work group, adopt a standard method of sideways printing, preferably using the same program. In this way, settings can be controlled, and worksheets of different users easily compared.

- Be careful about the legibility of any small print, especially if the printout is to be photocopied.

- To obtain the best possible results, consider the superior presentation quality afforded by a laser printer. (See Sections 13.5 and 13.6 on desktop publishing.)

13.5 DESKTOP PUBLISHING

Recent advances in laser printers and near-letter-quality (NLQ) dot matrix printers have made it possible for spreadsheet users

FIGURE 13-2 Printout using *Sideways* Printing Utility

```
Estate planning
Total liquid assets ......................................... E12
Net realizable value of non-liquid assets upon disposal
        House            E15    .8    E31*G31
        Other real estate E16   .8    E32*G32
        Automobile       E17    .7    E33*G33
        Jewelry          E18    .5    E34*G34
        Boat             E23    .6    E35*G35
                                      ─────────
            Net non-liquid asset value ..........    SUM(H31:H36)
Less: total liabilities ...............................    J24

    Realizable net worth .................................    J29+J37-J38
Monthly income level desired for the beneficiaries .......    3500
Number of years of monthly payment desired ...............    20
Expected average annual interest rate ....................    .1
Amount of capital required to sustain monthly income .....    ROUND(PV(J41,J43/12,J42*12),-1)
Life insurance premium required ..........................    J44-J40
Present life insurance coverage ..........................    85000
Excess (deficient) coverage ..............................    J45-J46
```

137

and developers to bring increasingly better quality to their printed work. Of particular interest is the high resolution made possible by the laser printer, for which a wide range of fonts is available.

A *font* is a set of letters, numbers, and other characters in a particular style and size of typeface. Some fonts also include a *line drawing* capability, which can be useful for forms or specialized reports. While most dot matrix and daisywheel printers are limited to two or three fonts such as Elite or Pica, desktop publishing methods offer a very large selection of fonts, and thus, many ways to bring a unique style to a spreadsheet presentation. Even with a little knowledge of desktop publishing, a spreadsheet developer can apply these tools skillfully to highlight different parts of the spreadsheet and to direct the reader's attention to the important aspects.

The golden rules of spreadsheet presentation, however, do not change with this technology. The spreadsheet must be easy to read and easy to understand. To achieve presentation quality, therefore, judicious use should be made of available fonts and other graphic techniques.

Some spreadsheet programs such as *Microsoft Excel* have built-in capabilities to take advantage of laser printing options and thereby print spreadsheets of superior quality. For other programs, add-in printing utilities may be available.

Example.

Figure 13–3 is the output from a *Lotus 1-2-3* worksheet using the add-in utility *Allways* from Funk Software. The printout was done with an HP LaserJet II printer. The *Allways* program add-in provides the user with a variety of fonts, colors, and formatting capabilities not found in *1-2-3*; it can also include graphs on the same page as a worksheet.

The title in Figure 13–3 is printed in Times 20 point; the subheading and column labels are in Times 14 point. The labels for cash receipts, cash disbursements, and cash excess (shortage) are set boldface to draw attention to these major categories. All numbers are formatted to Triumvirate 14 point. Instead of lines of dashes, *Allways* enables you to draw single and double continuous underlines.

13.6 GUIDELINES FOR DESKTOP PUBLISHING

Desktop publishing is as much an art as it is a science. The spreadsheet user new to this field will probably be making decisions

FIGURE 13–3 Printout Using *Allways* Add-in Utility

Westcoast Import and Export Inc.
Cash Flow Projection
From 1–Oct–89 to 31–Dec–89

	Oct 89	Nov 89	Dec 89
Sales	$113,400	$114,818	$116,253
Cash receipts:			
Collections from A/R	104,800	112,560	113,967
Interest income	0	125	0
Other cash receipts	5,000	6,000	9,000
Total cash receipts	109,800	118,685	122,967
Cash disbursements:			
Wages and salaries	60,000	55,000	69,000
Rent	10,000	10,000	10,000
Selling expenses	17,010	17,223	17,438
Advertising	12,000	11,000	15,000
Interest expense	43	0	25
Other expenses	15,000	13,000	14,000
Total cash disbursements	114,053	106,223	125,463
Cash excess (shortage)	($4,253)	$12,462	($2,496)

about the best use of typographic style for the first time. Formerly, such decisions would have been left to the graphic artist or the printer.

This new freedom of style can cause its own problems for the spreadsheet user. Commonly, the mistake is to employ too many different fonts and embellishments. The result can be visual clutter and confusion.

The following guidelines for effective desktop publishing with spreadsheets clarify some of the key choices to be made.

Fonts. Laser printers come with a selection of built-in, or *internal* fonts. Additional fonts may be obtained in two ways: by plugging *font cartridges* into the printer, or by using *soft fonts*. A font cartridge is a compact, miniature circuit board that stores the details of specific typefaces and sizes, and controls the appearance of printed characters. Soft fonts contain the same information, but in files on a conventional diskette rather than on a circuit board. The soft font carries the information about print images and formats to the printer.

All types of fonts increase the flexibility of dot matrix and laser printers. However, with laser printers you also have to be concerned with the memory capacity of the printer; font cartridges, being self-contained, do not draw on printer memory, but soft fonts do take up memory, both on the hard disk where they are stored and in the printer memory after they have been *downloaded*.

Diskettes containing soft fonts can be purchased from software developers, and the fonts are downloaded from the hard disk to the printer memory as required. It is possible to use hard and soft fonts in the same document.

Selecting fonts. Select only two or three different type styles for a spreadsheet. Often, a single style will be adequate. Some fonts come in a *font family* of compatible styles and are relatively easy to work with on a page; other fonts can be so different in their design that they create a visual clash that distracts the reader. Ideally, the reader should be virtually unaware of the fonts or the layout of the page. If the display is well done, the reader will only be aware of the content and, perhaps, the feeling that the spreadsheet is well presented.

Within a single font or font family, variety and emphasis can be achieved by:

- *Change in the size of the type.* Main headings can be of the same typeface but of a larger size than subheadings.

- *Use of all capitals for some headings or labels.* Be sparing in use of capitals. Although capitals add emphasis, they may be less legible than lower case letters, partly because the lower case letters with their "ascender" and "descender" strokes are easier to distinguish. Perhaps for this reason, spelling errors often creep into capitalized headings.

- *Use of boldface.* The visual impact of boldface is generally good for emphasis. Be selective in what you wish to emphasize.

- *Use of italics.* Italics signal to the reader that there is a change of pace or content. The "forward lean" of italics can change the visual balance of a page, but, again should be used sparingly.

Specialized terms used in descriptions of fonts and their use are shown in Table 13–1.

Lines. Lines are used in spreadsheets to punctuate the contents of a spreadsheet. Most spreadsheets containing financial information use single lines to mark the subtotal of a column of values, and double lines to denote the total. If these conventions are not followed, a reader could draw incorrect conclusions.

Boxes. Drawing boxes around items on a spreadsheet can be an effective way to direct the reader's attention. This is often a good way to visually separate and emphasize a range of cells for a particular purpose.

Shades. Some programs permit the background of spreadsheet cells to be shaded. This effect should be used only with great caution, and printed output should be checked for legibility. Shading may interfere with the display of the contents of cells; with some printers, shaded values may be illegible.

Color. Careful use of color can enhance spreadsheet presentation. While color will mainly be of interest for on-screen spreadsheets or graphics, there is an increasing use of color in printed spreadsheets, and color photocopying is becoming more common in centers of business. Color images generated on the microcomputer can also be projected directly to wall-size screens, or transcribed to overhead transparencies or slides.

Avoid using too many colors on a single page. Certain color combinations (such as white on blue) have greater readability than others (red on yellow). Also be aware of conventions and connotations about color. Negative values and losses are conventionally shown in red, so red should only be used this way on financial spreadsheets. Pastel tints might be appropriate in some con-

TABLE 13-1 Terms Used in Describing Fonts

Character set	The set of letters, numbers, symbols, and special line-drawing graphics included in a font. Examples: USASCII, Roman-8, Math, or Spanish.
Default	The font that will be printed if no overriding command is given.
Landscape orientation	The font prints along the length of the page. [See also Portrait.]
Pitch	The number of characters printed per inch horizontally (CPI). Pitch may be fixed (same spacing for all characters) or proportional (spacing varies depending on the natural width of each character). Examples: 12 pitch (12 characters to the inch), 15 or 17 pitch (also called compressed printing).
Point size	Height of characters in a font. There are 72 points to the inch. Examples: 8 point, 10 point, or 36 point.
Portrait orientation	The font prints across the width of a page. [See also Landscape.]
Spacing	Horizontal space occupied by letters. A special type of spacing called kerning adjusts spacing between pairs of letters for improved visual effect. [Do not confuse with line spacing, which is horizontal distance between lines.]
Style	Upright or italic slant.
Typeface	Name of the font. Examples: Courier, Helvetica, Times Roman, or Prestige Elite.
Weight	Thickness of the characters. Examples: light, medium, or bold.

texts, but other situations might demand a strictly black and white effect. Take care also to ensure that the intended reader does not have difficulty distinguishing color.

Given these precautions, desktop publishing techniques offer great potential for putting the finishing touch to a well designed spreadsheet. Why not help your spreadsheets travel in style!

CHAPTER 14

IN A FEW WORDS . . .

1. The consistent use of good spreadsheet style will significantly reduce the chance of error.
2. Planning starts with purpose. Think about the purpose of the spreadsheet. Tailor it to meet the purpose of the reader.
3. Block designs help you organize where to put the data and to remember where to find it.
4. Keep formulas simple, and enter variable data in a separate cell so they are easy to update without changing the formula.
5. Named ranges with meaningful names can improve spreadsheet readability if used sparingly.
6. Document essential facts about a spreadsheet on the file itself, and use cell notes to explain values or formulas.
7. Learn a few error-checking techniques, then routinely build them into your formulas.
8. Apply the decision power of the spreadsheet by appropriate use of the IF, CHOOSE, and LOOKUP functions.
9. Automate repetitive tasks with macros to save time and increase accuracy.
10. Use multiple, linked, or 3-D spreadsheets to manage related data stored on separate spreadsheets.
11. A spreadsheet can perform effectively as a database if the entry, retrieval, and reporting needs are straightforward.
12. Carefully select graph type and visual features to show trends, comparisons, and contrasts effectively from spreadsheet data.
13. Recognize that desktop publishing is an art. Be prepared to learn the art and craft of the trade.
14. Be accurate. Be readable. Be consistent.

Index